THE RUT HUNTERS

Pursuit of the WHITETAIL SLAM

TOM MIRANDA

Published by

Krause Publications, a division of F+W Media, Inc.
700 East State Street • Iola, WI 54990-0001
715-445-2214 • 888-457-2873
www.krausebooks.com

To order books or other products call toll-free 1-800-258-0929
or visit us online at www.shopdeerhunting.com

Cover photography by Kenny Bahr, Windigoimages.com

ISBN-13: 978-1-4402-3837-6
ISBN-10: 1-4402-3837-5

Cover Design by Sharon Bartsch and Dane Royer
Designed by Dane Royer
Edited by Chris Berens

Printed in China

Tom Miranda,
adventure bowhunter

DEDICATION

This book is dedicated to the excitement of the young hunter, whose pulse quickens at the sound of deer hooves on the forest floor.

Who experiences the uncontrollable tremble as a mature buck closes the distance.

And the rush of buck fever at that moment of truth.

For these emotions are not driven by inexperience, but by the passion that lures both the young... and the young at heart, to trek into wild places in pursuit of the magnificent white-tailed deer… and the very catalyst that insures we will always protect them.

TOM MIRANDA

CONTENTS

FOREWORD: WHY THE WHITETAIL IS KING

Most of us envision bugling elk, bug-eyed swaying bull moose responding to a plaintive call, or perhaps a few of the critters that call Africa home when we dream big about hunting. Even though our desires belong to animals beyond easy reach, our hearts belong to the whitetail, especially whitetail bucks.

It's their ability to make us feel like we don't belong in the woods that we secretly love. Despite oft-suppressed desires to hunt for "easy" bucks, the reality is that whitetail hunting exists as a delicate balance between challenge and potential success. It's the perfect pursuit because it demands nearly unrealistic optimism, which is often tempered by the very real feeling of eating another tag.

It would be easy enough to say that whitetails rule simply because they are so common. If that were true, we'd be watching fishing tournaments where professional anglers tried their hands at catching big limits of sunfish instead of bass or redfish. Commonality can sometimes detract from a species, but not the whitetail. Their availability to nearly every hunter is one of the reasons that they are so endearing to us.

TOM MIRANDA

Anyone can shoot a whitetail, right? After all it is not that hard to lay eyes on some deer if you know where to look. They are everywhere; they are not dumb. And they don't put up with our intrusion too well when we express a desire to turn them into tightly-wrapped packages of protein. They can be dumb, but those deer live in special circumstances, and you can bet a little predation would go a long way toward changing their habits forever.

It's deer of all shapes and sizes that have spawned a huge hunting industry, and the demand for know-how on all-things-deer have turned passionate hunters into businessmen. Our collective desire to figure out how to better kill deer has led to the creation of so many products that it would be impossible to count them all.

Those products – from state-of-the-art camouflage, to calls, to trail cameras, to you-name-it – are designed to make it easier to fill a tag, especially when it comes to big bucks. Some do, some don't. Even the best products that make it easier, don't make it that much easier because they simply can't change the nature of the animal we're after.

A mature buck is a no-nonsense critter that knows more about your habits than you do his, and he learned all of them through evidence of your intrusion. He feels more confident in the nighttime than he does in the day, and that's enough to get him to lay down and wait out the daylight hours. Sure, he'll get up and stretch and maybe browse for a while. But you can bet he'll have the wind in his favor, and his ears will constantly swivel to and fro to pick up the slightest sound that doesn't belong.

If you get to see him, you're lucky, however your job is far from over. Whitetail bucks grow big because they make it through encounters with hunters every year. They learn from those encounters that carelessness is dangerous, so they engage in less and less reckless behavior as they grow older. The only solace we can take in that is the rut – the short period of the year when mature deer sometimes throw caution to the wind and move during daylight with their minds on other needs beyond individual survival.

The whitetail is king for plenty of reasons. Tags are easy to get, they live in every kind of habitat you can imagine, and despite how hard it truly is, the chance to kill a genuine giant exists for every one of us.

What is not to love about that? God bless the whitetail.

Tom Miranda

INTRODUCTION

There may be others who are just as passionate about hunting whitetails as I am, but no one is more passionate than me. I have patterned my whole life around whitetail hunting. Born in Pennsylvania, raised in New England, educated in Indiana and living in Montana for close to thirty years, I've been a whitetail fanatic for over five decades. I presently reside in rural Iowa strictly for the quality whitetail opportunities found there.

Pursuing big whitetail bucks became an insatiable craving for quality hunting experiences. Living in the West, I was blessed to have upwards of 10 species of big game to pursue. But, for almost thirty years in Montana I spent 90 percent of my time strictly hunting whitetails. To date, I hunt for the personal satisfaction of close encounters. In order to extend my seasons I now hunt strictly with a bow and arrow, and have for many years. I don't own a shotgun, muzzleloader or even a .22. I prefer the close range limitations of a quality, traditional recurve bow shot instinctively. Frankly, I could care less what others shoot. I strongly desire the challenge yet still want to maintain a reasonable chance to attain my personal goals.

One of my biggest concerns for our future generations is that today's youths are straying away from woodsmanship skills. The hunting industry is turning hunting into shooting, with the thought being that "easier is supposedly better." I'm of the opinion there is no substitute for time spent in the woods through the application of practical experience. That alone will add to your understanding and ultimately your self-satisfaction. Become one with nature. Read the books, watch the videos, listen to the seminars, and then get into the woods and really learn. Your greatest weapon is your mind. Even though whitetails may be the ultimate challenge, we as humans are the masters of common sense, logic and reasoning. Think! It will add to your understanding, and ultimately you will more deeply appreciate the self-satisfaction derived from the results.

BARRY WENSEL

At some point you will probably reach a stage in your hunting life where you will not find it absolutely necessary to kill a deer. You might not believe me right now, but you will. It's a personal thing. I find myself passing up some bucks I probably should have shot, and shooting others that might not have been quite as big. The bottom line is I have my own reasons and adapt accordingly. It's all about self-satisfaction, personal desires and moods. We each need to decide what we want from a hunt – whether it's the challenge, the camaraderie, the fun, trophies, meat, or a combination of all of these and more.

I find myself developing a personal relationship with specific deer regardless of antler sizes. I admire the maturity and intelligence of older animals. Some of my favorite memories did not come from my largest bucks. I can live with that. In my opinion, that's the way God meant it to be.

So read this fine book and make your own decisions. Decide for yourself, and only yourself, what you want from this endeavor. Let the passion burn but be honest with yourself and others. Always maintain proper virtues, moral excellence and righteousness. It will be a decision you'll never regret as long as you live. Be thankful for our blessings and pursue our American freedoms at their finest.

Barry Wensel

CHAPTER 1

INTRODUCTION TO THE WHITETAILS OF NORTH AMERICA

by Dr. James C. Kroll

White-tailed deer (Odocoileus virginianus) have undergone two evolutions during their two or more million years of existence; the first began about 20 million years ago, the second only in the last few thousand years as they adapted to humans. The latter is what this book is really all about.

Understanding the origin of whitetails is critical both to management and hunting. It tells how and why our favorite game animal came to be, what it is and how it behaves. The story begins in an unlikely place, the tropical forests of Asia. About 50 million years ago, small omnivorous mammals developed specialized digestive systems consisting of four chambers. Ruminants, as they are called, were the "new kids on the block," with the ability to digest a wider array of plants. By the Pleistocene (2.5 million years ago), this group of mammals had exploded into a vast array of species, including the ancestors of deer (Cervidae). You would barely recognize these Asian cousins. They had no antlers and sported prominent fangs for protection and fighting. There are a few remnants still alive today, including the muntjac (Muntiacus reevesi), Chinese water deer (Hydropotes inermis), tufted deer (Elaphodus cephalophus) and musk deer (Moschus moschiferus).

Some time later, fangs gave way to hair-covered protrusions from the forehead. Current scientific thought is that these structures (ossicones) were developed to provide a surface for scent dispersal. Indeed, the muntjac has both fangs and antlers protruding from an elongated, hair-covered pedicle; perhaps a holdover from the ossicone condition.

Why was scent dispersal so important? Tropical forests are notoriously diverse in species, thus reducing the number of individuals in any one species. Because of this, early deer probably existed in low densities, creating difficulties in communication which therefore resulted in several adaptations caused by forest life. The well-known "grunt" of bucks uses low-pitched tones because they travel farther in a dense, wooded environment. The best way to communicate under such conditions is to have the ability to disperse scent and leave chemical messages. Again, this is important to the whitetail hunter, since bucks still leave such messages on signposts within staging areas where does congregate.

By the time deer reached North America, there were two types of antlers: those that arose from hair-covered structures that later stripped velvet to produce a permanent boney antler (Merycodonts); and those that lost the boney antler annually (Cervidae). Both of these animals appeared first in western North America, then over the next few million years, they spread southward and eastward throughout the continent, even reaching South America. No one knows what was the ancestor

Some prehistoric deer had fangs, others palmated antlers. North America's deer migrated across the Bering Land Bridge millions of years ago. Dr. Kroll believes that the first animal to look and act like the deer we know today was similar to the black-tailed deer living in the Pacific Northwest, and that both mule deer and white-tailed deer are direct descendents of blacktails.

(if there was one) of whitetails. I personally feel the black-tailed deer (Odocoileus hemionus columbianus) either is the oldest species in the genus or the actual ancestor to whitetails. DNA studies at Purdue University indicate blacktails and mule deer became separated by glaciers, leading to these two separate species. It probably occurred also with whitetails and the blacktail/mule deer group. I have no idea how long all of this took, but I do have a jawbone from a whitetail found in southern Florida that is 1.2 million years old. By the way, it was aged at over 6½ years of age – which makes you wonder just what kind of predators that deer had to avoid throughout its life...

By the time Lewis and Clark began their epic journey across North America, the Virginia deer (as they called them) had spread throughout the continent, into Mexico and Central America, and even reached Argentina as the South American Whitetail (Odocoileus virginianus cariacou). However, we now concede this group of whitetails has remained separated from other

Landowners today look at whitetails as a cash crop and grow them with the same passion as cattle, pigs, corn and soybeans.

subspecies long enough to be considered a new species (Odocoileus margaritae, O. lasiotis and O. cariacou). It's fascinating to imagine the vast array of habitats and conditions whitetails adapted to over the course of a few million years! Yet, the average whitetail hunter of today tends to think of this amazingly diverse species as a single animal, probably the only one he or she hunts annually. That is why I have urged hunters and trophy records organizations such as the Boone and Crockett and Pope and Young Clubs to give broader consideration; and that is why I was so thrilled when Tom Miranda approached me about promoting the Whitetail Slam.

THE SUBSPECIES OF WHITETAILS

The white-tailed deer is the one animal that should have the most museum material available for research. Yet, it is amazing to me that it is the one species that lacks depth of historical documentation and taxonomic study. Perhaps it is because the species is considered so common. There have been many attempts to identify the subspecies, including anatomical, behavioral and genetics (DNA and mDNA) studies. The most commonly used range map for subspecies was published in the Stackpole Book, White-tailed Deer: Ecology and Management, edited by my long-time friend Lowell K. Halls (now deceased). Almost 900 pages, this book presented everything we knew about deer at the time of its publication in 1984, but offered no explanation as to how the subspecies lines were produced. It also is not clear how many subspecies there actually are in North America – not to mention Central and South America – but we think there once were between 30 and 38 subspecies.

Body weights and habitats vary dramatically. Whitetails range in size from as much as 400 pounds to less than 75 pounds. Habitats range from near arctic conditions to deserts and tropical forests. Subspecies such as the Coues (pronounced "cows") deer reportedly can live without free water.

The taxonomy of whitetails is more than just the drawing of geographic lines and anatomical distinctions. It is about the habitats in which they live and the people who hunt them; which are far more important to me. Consider North, Central and South America comprise 8.3 percent of the world's land mass, and the distance over which whitetails evolved covers a whopping 8,699 miles! Whitetails truly are one of the most adaptable species on earth, all predetermined by experiences in the tropical forests of Asia so many millennia ago. So, let's have a look at the most common subspecies, which include those now recognized in the Slam. We start in the north and work to the southern U.S.

50 million years ago, the first ruminants developed. Today, deer belong to the group and have adapted handily to the presence of agricultural food sources like soybeans and corn.

and northern Mexico. Left out will be the rare and endangered subspecies, and most of the 13-14 subspecies in Mexico; some of which we are not even sure still exist.

COLUMBIAN WHITETAIL

The Columbian Whitetail (O. v. leucurus) has made a remarkable comeback since it was designated an endangered species, and was delisted in 2003 from the Federal List of Endangered and Threatened Species. My friend, Gordon Whittington, has been fortunate to hunt and harvest these beautiful, large-bodied deer inhabiting parts of Oregon and Washington. I had the chance to hunt them once and came away without a trophy, but with a great deal of respect. In my opinion, they are one of the most beautiful whitetails, often with double and triple throat patches and rich brown coloration. They are named for the Columbia River and the adjacent drainages around which they live. They differ biologically by not being able to breed until 18 months of age, and are only able to have a single fawn. The rut occurs from the first part of November into December.

Columbian whitetails are hunted much differently than most subspecies. Located in a region where western-style hunting traditions prevail, most of these deer are taken by hunters walking over the steep terrain, similar to the techniques used for mule deer and blacktails. To harvest a Columbian whitetail truly is an experience of a lifetime.

NORTHWEST, NORTHERN ROCKY MOUNTAIN OR IDAHO WHITETAIL

The Northwest Whitetail (O. v. ochrourus) also is a beautifully-colored subspecies and is a neighbor to the Columbian whitetails. Their range includes Idaho, western Montana, Oregon, Washington and Wyoming in the U.S.; Alberta and British Columbia in Canada. They are mountain inhabitants, more difficult to hunt than most of the subspecies. They live at elevations above 6,000 feet. I also have pursued these deer unsuccessfully, and can attest to the difficulty in hunting them. Also as evidence of their rarity, as of this writing the SCI book only has 484 typical and 106 nontypical entries. Hunting tactics primarily are the same as those used for mountain mule deer. They possess very large racks and have a strong tendency to have 6-by-6 frames. The rut is also from early November to mid-December.

NORTH AMERICAN SUBSPECIES

1. *O. v. virginianus* – Virginia white-tailed deer or Southern white-tailed deer
2. *O. v. acapulcensis* – Acapulco white-tailed deer (southern Mexico)
3. *O. v. borealis* – Northern (woodland) white-tailed deer (the largest and darkest white-tailed deer)
4. *O. v. carminis* – Carmen Mountains deer
5. *O. v. chiriquensis* – Chiriqui white-tailed deer (Panama)
6. *O. v. clavium* – Key Deer or Florida Keys white-tailed deer (Florida Keys)
7. *O. v. couesi* – Coues white-tailed deer or Arizona white-tailed deer
8. *O. v. dacotensis* – Dakota white-tailed deer or Northern plains white-tailed deer (most northerly distribution, rivals the Northern white-tailed deer in size)
9. *O. v. hiltonensis* – Hilton Head Island white-tailed deer
10. *O. v. leucurus* – Columbian white-tailed deer (Oregon and western coastal area)
11. *O. v. macrourus* – Kansas white-tailed deer
12. *O. v. mcilhennyi* – Avery Island white-tailed deer
13. *O. v. mexicanus* – Mexican white-tailed deer (central Mexico)
14. *O. v. miquihuanensis* – Miquihuan white-tailed deer (central Mexico)
15. *O. v. nelsoni* – Chiapas white-tailed deer (southern Mexico and Guatemala)
16. *O. v. nemoralis* – (Central America, round the Gulf of Mexico to Surinam further restricted from Honduras to Panama)
17. *O. v. nigribarbis* – Blackbeard Island white-tailed deer
18. *O. v. oaxacensis* – Oaxaca white-tailed deer (southern Mexico)
19. *O. v. ochrourus* – Northwest white-tailed deer or Northern Rocky Mountain white-tailed deer
20. *O. v. osceola* – Florida coastal white-tailed deer
21. *O. v. rothschildi* – Coiba Island white-tailed deer
22. *O. v. seminolus* – Florida white-tailed deer
23. *O. v. sinaloae* – Sinaloa white-tailed deer (mid-western Mexico)
24. *O. v. taurinsulae* – Bulls Island white-tailed deer
25. *O. v. texanus* – Texas white-tailed deer
26. *O. v. truei* – Central American white-tailed deer (Costa Rica, Nicaragua and adjacent states)
27. *O. v. thomasi* – Mexican Lowland white-tailed deer
28. *O. v. toltecus* – Rain Forest white-tailed deer (southern Mexico)
29. *O. v. venatorius* – Hunting Island white-tailed deer
30. *O. v. veraecrucis* – Northern Vera Cruz white-tailed deer
31. *O. v. yucatanensis* – Yucatán white-tailed deer

8
10
19
3
11
1
25
24
29
9
17
7
12
20
22
4
6
14
30
28
31
23
13
27
16
2
15
18
26
5
21

DAKOTA WHITETAIL

The Dakota Whitetail (O. v. dacotensis) is one of my real favorites, occupying mostly prairie habitat, but also northern boreal forest, tiaga and scrublands of four Canadian provinces and five U.S. states. I spent 23 years of my career pursuing these deer, and some of my greatest hunts have involved these monster bucks. In fact, I once harvested a Dakota whitetail just about as far north as you possibly can on the edge of the tundra of Alberta. I am pretty confident in saying they probably are the largest-bodied subspecies.

Dakota whitetails could be the toughest deer when it comes to survival. They annually endure some of the worst winter conditions of any deer, from deep snowpacks to temperatures often considerably below -50°F. It has been rewarding to watch hunting tactics change since I first ventured to Alberta in the early 1980s. In those days, hunters generally drove around in pickups or did "pushes" through the bush to harvest a buck. Later, my friend Dave Bzway (Alberta Wilderness Guide Service) would set the standard for hunting these deer by employing advanced scouting and patterning techniques for ambush-style hunting.

If you are going to hunt Dakota whitetails, you might want to consider investing in quality cold weather gear. I personally have endured all-day hunts at -30°F on open tripod stands. These deer are well adapted to the cold, weighing in at more than 300 pounds. Dakotas seem to have benefited from grain farming and are most abundant in the fringe habitat where the northern forest and farmlands meet. The rut occurs in mid-November.

BOREAL (NORTHERN WOODLAND) WHITETAIL

To the east of the Dakota whitetail lives yet another beautiful subspecies, the Boreal Whitetail (O. v. borealis). Boreal means "of the north," referring to the climatic zone south of the Arctic. Yet another large subspecies, with a record reported weight of 354 pounds, their distribution is restricted to states and provinces around the Great Lakes and of the north Atlantic Ocean. The southern limit occurs at the banks of the Mississippi and Ohio rivers, although I don't understand how rivers can be limiting. To be honest, I feel this subspecies actually occurs farther south of Cairo, Ill. into the Mississippi River Delta. These are true for-

Modern farming practices continue to create habitat that proliferates white-tailed deer numbers.

The ability of a whitetail doe to disappear right in front of your eyes is one of the reasons they, as a species, have proliferated so well throughout the United States, Canada and Mexico.

TONY J PETERSON

est animals occupying both coniferous and deciduous habitat types. The rut occurs around the first two weeks of November.

The Boreal whitetail probably has as much hunting tradition associated with it as any deer subspecies. These are the deer of the northern hunting camp traditions, typical of states such as Wisconsin and Michigan. It also is the subspecies that has produced the most Boone and Crockett Club record book bucks.

VIRGINIA WHITETAIL

The Virginia Whitetail (O. v. virginianus) is the species first described in 1780 by a German naturalist named Eberhardt Zimmermann. Eastern American Indian tribes relied heavily on these deer for food and clothing, and even "managed" the forest using fire to produce more deer. They also were the first deer to be over-hunted to near extinction by 1900. They prefer a variety of habitats, but thrive in association with humans and agriculture. However, they are basically a southern forest dwelling subspecies. As their name implies, they are found from Virginia southward to

TONY J PETERSON

Few hunters understand the evolutionary process that has resulted in modern whitetails. The 50-million-plus year journey is truly impressive and has created a group of animals that has endeared itself to the hearts of hunters.

HUNTER BIO DR. JAMES KROLL

DR JAMES KROLL

AGE/HOMETOWN:
66/Nacogoches, Texas

YEARS HUNTING: 42 years

FAVORITE HUNT LOCATION:
Alberta, Canada

DEER HARVESTED:
Well over 1,000

LARGEST BUCK:
256 inches, 305 pounds

FAVORITE METHOD:
Rattling and calling

CONTACT INFO:
www.drdeer.com
www.northamericanwhitetail.com

WHITETAIL SLAM:
Yes, but not registered

Hunters tend to have a myopic view of the whitetails they are most familiar with. But if they could trace the lineage of a single deer, like this bedded Iowa doe, they'd be shocked to see how far whitetails have traveled, and how much they evolved to become the subspecies we hunt today.

northern Florida, and westward to the Ohio and Mississippi rivers.

Virginia whitetails are also part of a rich hunting tradition, and originally were pursued with hounds. Hound hunting remains, but has been reduced due to hunting restrictions and increasing human populations. Today, hunting tactics focus on ambush hunting from trees or blinds. They are probably the most benefited by food plots of any subspecies. This subspecies also offers the earliest hunting dates, with South Carolina opening in August. The rut occurs from October to December, decreasing from north to south in timing.

KANSAS WHITETAIL

The Kansas Whitetail (O. v. macrourus) has been associated with the state bearing its name, but historically has occurred from eastern Texas, northern Louisiana, and northward through Arkansas, Missouri and Iowa. Technically they only occur in eastern Kansas, but most hunters think of them being in western Kansas, where the next subspecies (Texas Whitetails) occur. The range also includes eastern Oklahoma and Nebraska.

As their scientific name implies, they have larger tails than most whitetails, giving them the local name "flags." In my opinion, they rank among the most handsome of deer, with grizzled coats and faces. Their antlers are disproportionately large for their body size. Preferred habitats include both forests and prairies, as well as brushlands.

I have spent a significant amount of time hunting these deer. In 1987, I was fortunate to kill one of the biggest whitetails that year from the last remaining population of Kansas whitetails in eastern Texas (Boggy Slough); he was lured to the grunt call and had enormous 9 inch bases, and four drop tines. The rut generally is complete by the middle of November; Kansas schedules its rifle season to occur after the rut. Hunting methods include stalking and ambush hunting, but I prefer rattling, calling and decoys. Kansas whitetails occupy one of the last "new places" for trophy whitetails – along with Iowa, eastern Oklahoma and Nebraska. If there ever is a new world record whitetail, it will come from this subspecies and one of these places, although Wisconsin cannot be taken for granted.

The difference in antler growth between young bucks in varying regions is staggering. Bucks in the South Central Plains and Woodlands regions may sport six- or eight-point racks, while others in the Gulf Coast or Seminole regions may remain spikes or forkhorns much later in life due to poor soil quality and food nutrition.

TEXAS WHITETAIL

This subspecies' range extends from northern Mexico, throughout Texas, and northward into western Oklahoma, eastern New Mexico, Colorado, western Kansas and Nebraska. Texas Whitetails (O. v. texanus) are known to have statistically wider antler spreads than any other subspecies. Although commonly associated with the South Texas brush country, this subspecies has a wide array of habitat preferences, but generally can be described as a brushland group of deer.

Texas whitetail hunting tactics gave us antler rattling, probably the most exciting way to harvest a buck. This also is the subspecies from which modern quality deer management arose, and many of the management practices such as culling, supplementation and restricted buck harvest can be associated with Texas whitetails. I grew up hunting this subspecies. This is a subspecies that unfortunately has been genetically altered in Texas by stockings of the next subspecies, the Avery Island Whitetail. As a consequence in much of Texas the rut is variable. Where there are pure Texas whitetails, however, the rut occurs during mid-November in the southeastern and northern portions of their range, to mid-December in the southwestern portion and northeastern Mexico.

AVERY ISLAND WHITETAILS

A smaller subspecies, these deer derive both their common and scientific names (O. v. mcilhennyi) from the land of Tabasco – Avery Island, La., and the McIlhenney family. These light-colored deer occupy primarily swamp and marshlands from just north of Corpus Christi, Texas, to the swamps around New Orleans, La. They are difficult to hunt due to the habitat they prefer, but offer a great challenge. They seldom achieve antlers scoring more than 130 inches, B&C. But, I consider them to be one of the most fascinating deer I have successfully hunted. One of the most interesting things about them is that their rut occurs in late September to early October, making them a great early season choice for your hunting season.

CARMEN MOUNTAIN WHITETAIL

Wild and woolly would be the best description of my hunts for Carmen Mountain Whitetails (O. v. carminis). These diminutive mountain and deep-brush dwellers are the least known of huntable deer on our list. They live in some of what can be considered the last wilderness in North America, just north and south of the Rio Grande River of Texas and Mexico. I have been fortunate enough to harvest one of these deer, and it was not easy! I am still not convinced they are simply an eastern version of the Coues deer, as there are some significant differences. For example, they seem to depend on free water more than Coues; hence, the best strategy is to ambush them at water. Their rut is late December to mid-January, giving you an excellent subspecies to hunt late in the year.

A young spike buck sneaks through the northwoods of Minnesota. Whitetails are found in many different subgroups throughout their current range and they inhabit some amazingly different types of habitat.

COUES DEER

You already have endured my obsession with the pronunciation of Coues deer ("cows") (O. c. couesi). These are small, mountainous desert and high forest deer, which are very difficult to kill at close range. Their range extends from central Mexico into Arizona and New Mexico. Hunting strategies include glassing mountainsides and long shots with a rifle. Bow kills are possible on the rare occasions they come to water. Their rut is usually in late December to early January. A really good Coues deer will score in the low 100s, but who really cares? This is one of the "must haves" of the Slam!

Dr. Deer, James Kroll, has taken plenty of whitetails in his day, including some absolute giants.

FLORIDA SUBSPECIES

I include the Florida subspecies as a group, because they are so different from all the others. These are subtropical to tropical subspecies, often behaving more like tropical deer species in their breeding habits. They also have spawned some of the most unique hunting techniques and traditions of all the North American subspecies.

The Florida Coastal Whitetail (O. v. osceola) inhabits the swamps and pine forests of the eastern Gulf Coast of Florida, southward to the central part of the state. If you really like eastern diamondback rattlers and cottonmouths, you will love hunting Florida Coastal Whitetails! There are many unique things about this subspecies, but one is the low nutritional quality of the natural deer foods due to climatic and soil conditions. As a consequence, bucks may have spikes well into their life before reaching peak antler size. Hound hunting is a tradition in this region, but ambush hunting has grown in popularity. The unique habitat and hunting traditions make this subspecies a good one to consider. The rut in northwestern Florida for this subspecies probably includes February and March.

I have been blessed to manage deer throughout their range, and have considerable experience with our last subspecies, the Seminole Whitetail (O. v. seminolus). These are southern Florida deer that might as well have webbed feet because they live in stark, swamp-dominated tropical habitats that in parts of the year are desert-dry and at other times flooded. They are the prime prey of the Florida panther and black bear, along with a host of predators including coyotes and bobcats; not to mention alligators. As if they are not unique enough, their rut occurs sporadically – including June and July. It is common to see spotted fawns as early as

Dr. James Kroll probably understands more about the evolution of white-tailed deer than anyone. His research is aided by a love of whitetails and the burning desire to hunt them any chance he can.

February. Since the season runs from the first of August to early January, the rut never is included in the season. Hunting traditions are varied, ranging from hounds to swamp buggies.

SUMMARY

As you begin this book, I hope this chapter has given you a much greater appreciation for our favorite game species. The natural history of whitetails began in the steamy tropics of Asia and spread eastward into North, Central and South America. Along the way, whitetails adapted to a staggering array of habitats and climates, changing to fit the needs for survival. Over the last few thousand years of their existence, we have seen a concomitant evolution in hunting tactics and traditions by humans. It was my goal in writing this introduction to give you a far greater appreciation for whitetails than just the size of their antlers. I sincerely hope the next stage in hunting evolution will be focused more on gaining new experiences and appreciation of different deer subspecies and their habitats. Good hunting!

CHAPTER 2

BIG GAME ACCOMPLISHMENTS

In North America, the white-tailed deer is king. Studies have shown over 12 million hunters pursue whitetails, and the pursuit of these magnificent animals generates billions of dollars in our economy.

In today's society, hunters engage in big-game hunting as a recreational pastime. All big-game animals that are taken should be eaten, even though the food value of wild game is often looked on as a bonus to the completion of a successful hunt. Gone are the days when men took to the field to secure meat for the family. Farming and raising livestock has replaced sustenance hunting and most trophy whitetailers eat chicken, steak, pork and seafood along with their venison.

THE RECORD BOOKS

The recreational aspect of hunting big game has created a pseudo competition between hunter and game. Record books now exist that list the measured antlers, horns and skulls of mature bucks, bulls, rams, billies and boars. Hunting organizations proliferate sport hunting and track hunter accomplishments. Members pay a fee to register their animal's score to be listed in each record book. The highest all-time score for each species is known as the "world record," and record books exist that separate the accomplishments between rifle, muzzleloader, pistol, compound bow, traditional bow and crossbow.

Many trophy hunters go afield with an eye to the record books.

The challenge of shooting a whitetail buck that makes the record book can be a fantastic personal goal. Bowhunters submitting entries for the Pope and Young record book must meet 125 inches for a typical-antlered whitetail buck, which must be harvested with archery equipment. The Boone and Crockett minimum is 170 inches typical for whitetails taken with firearms. Nontypical-antlered bucks are categorized differently and demand higher minimums. Both of these books use a measuring system that deducts inches for a lack of symmetry, thus they necessitate both a gross and a net score. Gross score is total inches before deductions, and net score is after deductions. Only the net scores are used in the B&C and P&Y record books.

Safari Club International also administers a record book for its members. SCI's record book is the largest in the world and utilizes a scoring system that operates with gross total inches. SCI also recognizes all of the huntable big-game species of the world, unlike B&C and P&Y who recognize only North American species.

Buckmasters also operates a whitetail record book for its members entitled Buckmasters Trophy Records, or BTR. This system began in 1994 and is similar to the

JIM SHOCKEY

Hunting icon Jim Shockey has earned the GSCO's Grand Slam and Super Slam as well as SCI's prestigious World Hunting award. Jim is a big advocate of documenting his hunting heritage

DR. JOHN "JACK" FROST

Tom Miranda poses with a great Kansas whitetail.

DR. JOHN "JACK" FROST

LEFT: Dr John "Jack" Frost was the first bowhunter to harvest an archery Grand Slam® of wild sheep. This fireplace photo taken in Frost's home shows his collective wild sheep Slam. ABOVE: Jack Frost poses with a great desert bighorn sheep taken on Carmen Island, Mexico.

SCI system of measuring antlers, yet does not include an "inside spread" measurement. The thought process with the BTR is that only antler length and girth count to the score, and width is a measurement of "air" and not antler.

There are other big-game record books as well. Rowland Ward began measuring African species in the late 1800s, and his first record book was released in 1892. European hunters often use the CIC trophy measuring and monitoring system established in the mid 1930s. Hunters in New Zealand and Australia use the Douglas scoring system established in 1949.

Many hunters who harvest whitetail bucks enter their trophies in the record books. A buck that scores 190 inches gross typical may score 175 net typical, and if harvested with a bow could be entered in the Pope and Young Club book as 175. This same deer would score 190 in the SCI record book. That same buck's BTR score might be 170 if the inside spread was 20 inches. There are many intricate details to each scoring system, and every big-game record book requires a respective "official measurer" from the organization to record and verify the trophy. As this writing, a hunter must be a member of each organization (with the exception of the Pope and Young Club) to enter scores into its book, and costs differ per organization.

THE SLAMS

Slams are collections of animal species or subspecies. The most well known Slam is the wild sheep Grand Slam, which is the harvesting of one ram from each of the four subspecies of North American wild sheep. This accomplishment started in 1956 when mountain hunter Bob Housholder began circulating a newsletter to big-game hunters. Housholder's Grand Slam Club quickly gained popularity and started archiving hunting reports from hunters who were actively pursuing the different sheep subspecies. Grand Slam Club/Ovis, or GSCO, recognizes the harvesting of a Dall ram, a Stone or Fannin ram, a Desert Bighorn ram and a Rocky Mountain or California Bighorn ram as a GRAND SLAM® lifetime achievement. GSCO also

HUNTER BIO — TOM MIRANDA

AGE/HOMETOWN: 55 / Englewood, Fla.

YEARS HUNTING: Over 35 years

FAVORITE HUNT LOCATION:
Illinois, Kansas and Texas

DEER HARVESTED:
60-plus bow bucks on video

LARGEST BUCK:
174 inches, 14 points and 175 pounds

FAVORITE METHOD:
Treestand bowhunting and rattling in late October.

CONTACT INFO:
www.tommiranda.com
Territories Wild TV show,
Adventure Bowhunter book and DVD set- the first documented video Super Slam®

WHITETAIL SLAM: Yes

Muncho Lake, BC
OUTFITTERS
POPE & YOUNG CLUB
Tom Miranda
FL
BOWHUNTING
Big Game Records of North America

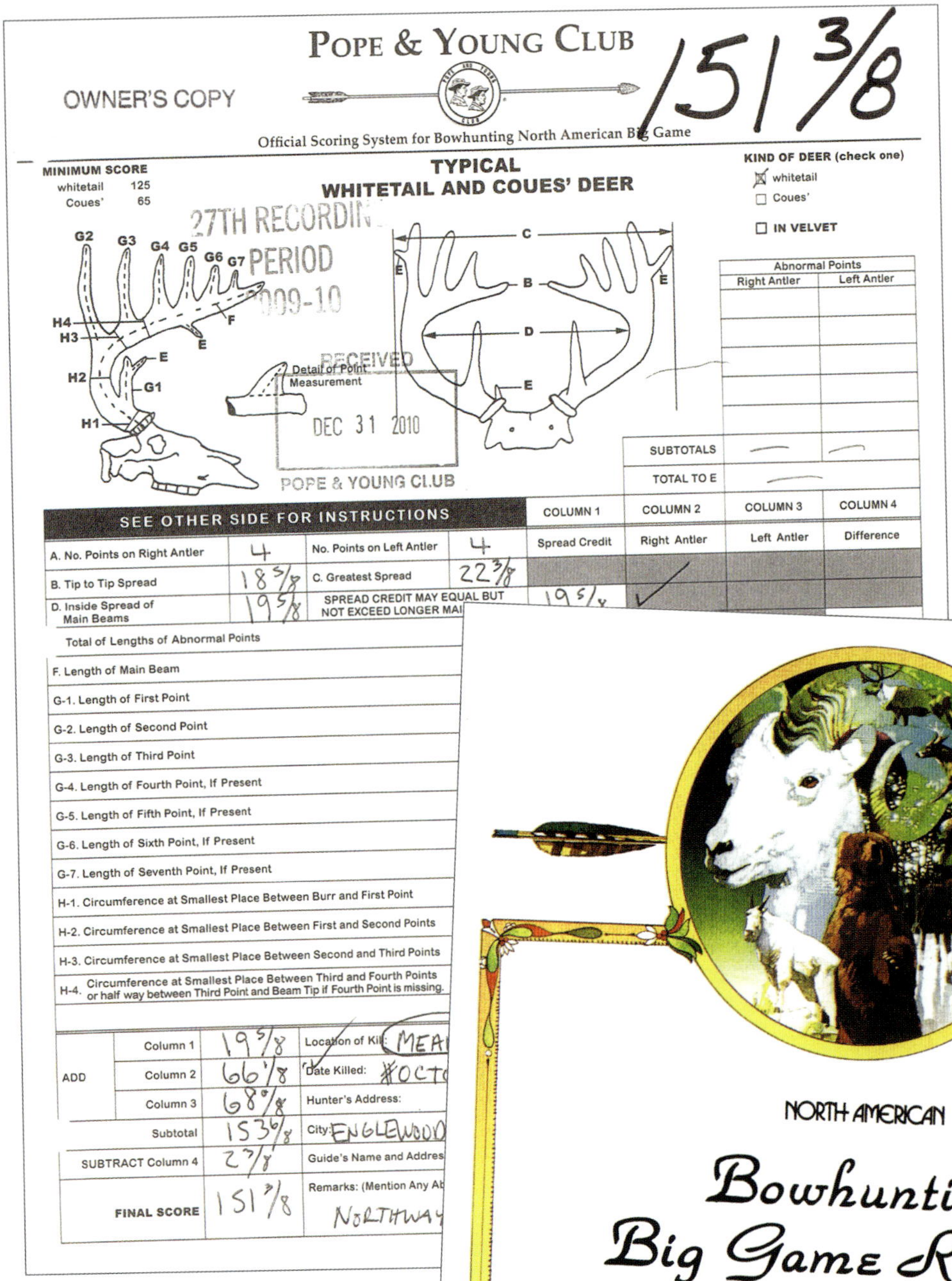
POPE & YOUNG CLUB
OWNER'S COPY
151 3/8
Official Scoring System for Bowhunting North American Big Game
MINIMUM SCORE
whitetail 125
Coues' 65
TYPICAL
WHITETAIL AND COUES' DEER
KIND OF DEER (check one)
whitetail
Coues'
IN VELVET
27TH RECORDING PERIOD 2009-10
RECEIVED
DEC 31 2010
POPE & YOUNG CLUB
Detail of Point Measurement
Abnormal Points
Right Antler
Left Antler
SUBTOTALS
TOTAL TO E
SEE OTHER SIDE FOR INSTRUCTIONS
COLUMN 1
COLUMN 2
COLUMN 3
COLUMN 4
Spread Credit
Right Antler
Left Antler
Difference
A. No. Points on Right Antler 4
No. Points on Left Antler 4
B. Tip to Tip Spread 18 5/8
C. Greatest Spread 22 3/8
D. Inside Spread of Main Beams 19 5/8
SPREAD CREDIT MAY EQUAL BUT NOT EXCEED LONGER MAI
Total of Lengths of Abnormal Points
F. Length of Main Beam
G-1. Length of First Point
G-2. Length of Second Point
G-3. Length of Third Point
G-4. Length of Fourth Point, If Present
G-5. Length of Fifth Point, If Present
G-6. Length of Sixth Point, If Present
G-7. Length of Seventh Point, If Present
H-1. Circumference at Smallest Place Between Burr and First Point
H-2. Circumference at Smallest Place Between First and Second Points
H-3. Circumference at Smallest Place Between Second and Third Points
H-4. Circumference at Smallest Place Between Third and Fourth Points or half way between Third Point and Beam Tip if Fourth Point is missing.
ADD
Column 1 19 5/8
Column 2 66 1/8
Column 3 68 0/8
Subtotal 153 6/8
SUBTRACT Column 4 2 3/8
FINAL SCORE 151 3/8
Location of Kill: MEA
Date Killed: OCTO
Hunter's Address:
City: ENGLEWOOD
Guide's Name and Addres
Remarks: (Mention Any Ab
NORTHWAY

NORTH AMERICAN
Bowhunting
Big Game Records
TYPICAL WHITETAIL DEER
SPECIES
151 3/8
SCORE
MEADOW LAKE, SASKATCHEWAN
WHERE TAKEN
OCTOBER 15, 1998
DATE
TOM MIRANDA
BOWHUNTER
THE POPE AND YOUNG CLUB
Roger W. Atwood
PRESIDENT
Mike Kistler
RECORDS CHAIRMAN

Tom Miranda with his 1998 Saskatchewan whitetail and the P&Y scoresheet & certificate (left) which archives the eight-point brute into the Pope and Young record book.

differentiates between archery and firearm Grand Slams, as well as the women who achieve this hunting milestone.

There are many other types of slams. A Wild Turkey Grand Slam is recognized by the National Wild Turkey Federation and includes four birds: legally taken Eastern, Merriam, Rio Grande and Osceola gobblers. A Royal Slam is a Turkey Grand Slam adding a Gould's gobbler from Mexico.

A SUPER SLAM® is the harvesting of North America's 29 big-game animals. It's is a collection of slams that include the wild sheep GRAND SLAM®, a deer slam, bear slam, elk slam, caribou slam, moose slam and the unique animals. The list of super slam animals includes: The deer – whitetail, Coues, mule, sitka black-tailed, Columbia black-tailed. The caribou – barren ground, mountain, central Canadian, Quebec / Labrador, woodland. The sheep – Dall, Stone, bighorn, desert bighorn. The bears – polar, black, grizzly, Alaskan brown. The moose – Alaskan / Yukon, Canadian, Shiras. The elk – rocky mountain, Roosevelt, tule. The uniques – bison, musk oxen, cougar, mountain goat and pronghorn. The Super Slam is recognized and archived by Grand Slam Club/Ovis, and is known as the most coveted big-game slam on the planet.

The Grand Slam Club/OVIS also archives and records world sheep and goat Slams. The OVIS SLAM Award is presented to a hunter who has taken 12 of the world's wild sheep. Since there are over 40 species and subspecies of wild sheep, OVIS also recognizes hunters who take 20 or 30 different sheep with the OVIS Super 20 and Super 30 awards. The Capra Award covers the world's wild goats with 12 animals being a CAPRA SLAM, CAPRA Super 20 includes twenty animals and Super 30, thirty animals.

Safari Club International is the king of big-game slams and hunter recognition. The club recognizes no less than 17 slams and 34 pinnacles of achievement, all of which allow SCI members who collect big-game species to be recognized. The depth of the award platforms for hunters at SCI is worldwide, and brackets the awards by continent as well as species groups. Slams

Tom Miranda's Whitetail Slam certificate.

are completed when a select number of animals are harvested from a list of eligible species. Pinnacles are completed in stages ranging from copper, bronze, silver, gold and diamond levels. One of SCI's highest achievements is the World Hunting Award – which requires 11 Slams and 17 Pinnacles of Achievement at diamond level, as well as qualifying for a fourth pinnacle and Crowning Achievement.

THE WHITETAIL SLAM

Since whitetails are the number one big-game animal hunted in the world, it's no wonder that there should be a whitetail slam. Yet, other than SCI's "Grand Slam of Whitetails" award, no other organization has stepped up to honor hunters who travel North America to hunt its extremely diverse whitetail population. Biologists have haggled for years over whitetail subspecies – some expanding the list to nearly 40 while others are content with less than 20. The proliferation of white-tailed deer has included much restocking, which has watered down the gene pool of true subspecies in most areas of North America. Since the white-tailed deer is by far the most biologically studied mammal on the planet, developing a slam of whitetails that contains animals that are truly different required some serious forethought as well as flexibility.

Renowned whitetail biologists Dr. Harry Jacobson, Dr. James Kroll, and QDMA biologists Brian Murphy and Kip Adams looked at the deer biology, habitat diversity and regional differences of North America's whitetail population to determine the eight subgroups of white-tailed deer recognized in the Whitetail SLAM®.

These respected deer scientists looked deeply into the whitetail's adaptation to local habitat, as well as the historical record of whitetails originally found in those areas before restocking. Harvest records also helped indicate deer size and antler growth characteristics that would differentiate one territory population from another.

Another key ingredient to defining a territory was the rut cycle data that helped to support the notion that the whitetails found in the different territories had

SAFARI CLUB INTERNATIONAL

SCI

FIRST FOR HUNTERS

Method 17-T Entry Form

For white-tailed deer with typical antlers. *Antlers that have one or more non-typical tines may be measured as typical at the owner's request, but only the typical tines will count in the score. Any non-typical tines are to be recorded as supplemental information.*

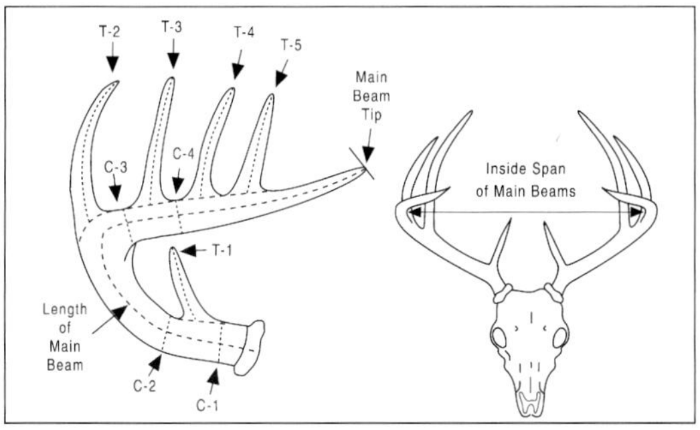

Hunter ______________________
How you want your name to appear in the Record Book

Membership No. ____________ e-mail ____________

Address ______________________

City ______ State ______ Zip ______ Country ______

Ph. (___) ______ Home (___) ______ Business (___) ______ Fax

I certify that, to the best of my knowledge, I took this animal without violating the wildlife laws or ethical hunting practices of the country or province in which I hunted. I also certify that, to the best of my knowledge, the laws of my country have not been violated by my taking or importing this animal.

Free-ranging ☐ Yes ☐ No

Signature ______________________

The acceptance or denial of all entries are at the discretion of Safari Club International, its Board and committees. Entries are subject to review by the Trophy Records Committee of SCI at any time. All photos and entries subitted to SCI become SCI's property.

Submit to: Safari Club International
4800 W. Gates Pass Rd., Tucson, AZ 85745 USA.

☐ **$35** Record Book processing fee
☐ **$55** Medallion Award processing fee *(Walnut plaque)* includes shipping & handling
☐ **$80** Record Book & Medallion Award processing fee includes shipping & handling

To enter Record Book and/or Medallion:

1) Add the appropriate entry processing fees together as necessary. *(Medallion fee includes shipping & handling.)*
2) All entries must be complete, signed by hunter and accompanied by fees and a photograph of the trophy.
3) Please clearly label back of photo with name of hunter, name and score of animal, and date taken.
☐ For simple horns and unbranched antlers: include 1 photo
☐ For animals with branched antlers: include enough photos so that all tines can be clearly seen.

Checks on U.S. banks only. Credit cards preferred. Entry fees are valid for 12 months from date of form located in lower right hand corner.

We Accept: ☐ MC ☐ Visa ☐ AMX ☐ Discover ☐ Diners Club

______ Card Number ______ Expiration Date

Animal ______________________

Remeasurement? ☐ Yes ☐ No Former Score ______ Record No. ______

Date Taken ______ Month ______ Day ______ Year

☐ Rifle ☐ Handgun ☐ Muzzleloader ☐ Bow ☐ Crossbow ☐ Picked Up

Place Taken ______ Country ______ State or Province

Locality ______________________

Guide ______________ Hunting Co. ______________

		L	R
I. Length of Main Beam		/8	/8
II. Length of Typical Tines	T-1	/8	/8
(Use back of form for additional tines)	T-2	/8	/8
	T-3	/8	/8
	T-4	/8	/8
	T-5	/8	/8
	T-6	/8	/8
	T-7	/8	/8
	Subtotal	0 0/8	0 0/8
III. Circumference of Main Beam	C-1	/8	/8
	C-2	/8	/8
	C-3	/8	/8
	C-4	/8	/8
	Subtotal	0 0/8	0 0/8
IV. Inside Span of Main Beams			/8
V. Total Score			0 0/8

Supplemental Information

		L	R
Length of non-typical tines, if any. (Not to be included in total score)	NT-1	/8	/8
	NT-2	/8	/8
	NT-3	/8	/8
	NT-4	/8	/8
Number of Typical Points (All typical tines plus beam tip)		0	0
Number of Non-typical Points (All non-typical tines)		0	0
Total Number of Points (All tines plus beam tip)		0	0

Official Measurer ______________________

Measurer No. ______________ Email ______________

Day Measured ______ Month ______ Day ______ Year

Signature of Measurer ______________________

For Office Use Only

Date Received: ______________________

 6/07

SCI score sheet.

Tom Miranda presents Grand Slam Club director Dennis Campbell his Super Slam award milestone.

adapted to climate and habitat, which modified breeding times and the proliferation of that specific population.

The eight SLAM territories all include more than one subspecies of white-tailed deer, yet for the purpose of a Whitetail SLAM, the territory boundaries encompass deer that as a group, live in similar habitat, with similar characteristics and rut cycles.

Whitetail SLAM territories include the Northern Woodlands, Southeastern, Dakota, South Central Plains, Gulf Coast, Northwestern, Coues and Seminole. A Whitetail SLAM hunter accomplishment is the harvesting of four unique bucks, one from each of four different subgroup territories. Hunters who harvest and register their bucks earn a Whitetail SLAM® certificate, and as members pursuing a slam are entitled to benefits like gear and hunt giveaways that are available at the organization's website.

An Ultimate Whitetail SLAM is the harvesting of a whitetail buck in all eight territories, and is recognized with a beautifully framed certificate. As any hunter who has traveled to hunt whitetails knows, success on mature bucks can be difficult. Since each Whitetail SLAM territory is so different and the territories cover nearly the entire continent, the Ultimate Whitetail SLAM is an incredible accomplishment.

SLAM BOUNDARIES

For most hunters who live or hunt on the boundaries of these areas, the deer found on both sides are seemingly one in the same. Just like northern British Columbia's coastal grizzlies resemble Alaskan brown bears – they aren't classified the same – even though bears walk from Alaska to British Columbia without a passport. The Columbia black-tailed deer territory is defined by a highway boundary and certainly deer cross this highway. Animal subspecies are often bracketed by the locations of their known home ranges, yet true boundaries are subject to change based on animal dispersion. Interbreeding between subspecies also can dilute the gene pool of animals whose ranges diverge. The boundaries are only a guide to help differentiate the subgroups.

THE CHALLENGE

Since most whitetail hunters have access to deer in their home state, most hunters target resident deer. With each Whitetail SLAM territory encompassing many states and provinces, hunters in pursuit of a SLAM will need to travel and hunt outside of their home territory.

Both Minnesota and Colorado residents have a unique situation in the habitat diversity of their states within the North American whitetail's range. Both states offers three different subgroups of deer, offering creative hunters a chance at a ¾ slam with a resident hunting license! Part of Minnesota lies in each of the Northern Woodlands, South Central Plains and Dakota subgroups. Colorado harbors the Dakota, South Central Plains and Northwestern subgroups.

The ring of counties that touch the Gulf of Mexico also give the Gulf Coast states two whitetail subgroups, and allow resident hunters the opportunity at half of a slam within their own state.

Success when traveling to hunt whitetails is never a sure thing and often relies on many outside influences such as moon phase, weather, rut timing and more. Since most traveling hunters operate with a limited amount of hunting days, it's easy to see that a stretch of bad weather can ruin even the best laid plans. Whitetails are also notoriously finicky and will lay up in warm weather. Many top whitetail hunters hunt their home areas during the early and late season when deer are on patternable feeding cycles. Then they travel outside of their home area to hunt other whitetail subgroups during the rut when mature deer are moving, and opportunities increase to intercept bucks searching, chasing and breeding estrus does.

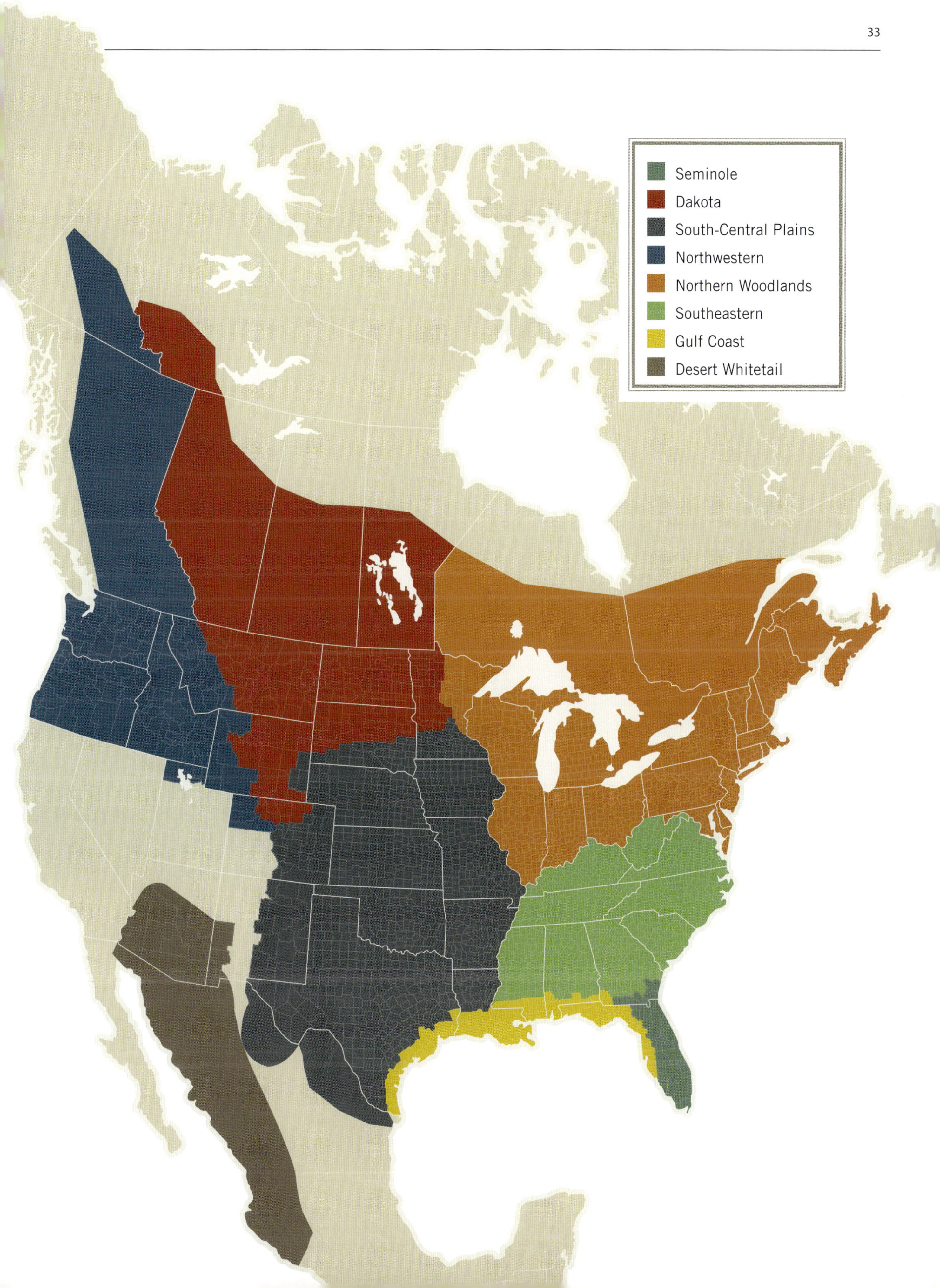
Seminole
Dakota
South-Central Plains
Northwestern
Northern Woodlands
Southeastern
Gulf Coast
Desert Whitetail

Mr. Whitetail™ Larry Weishuhn with an incredible Southeastern buck taken in Kentucky near the Ohio river. There's no question that whitetail genetics mix in areas close to the SLAM territory boundaries.

LARRY WEISHUHN

Georgia bowhunter Jason Sebo scores out of state at Carters Hunting Lodge in Pike County, Illinois.

GET INVOLVED

Becoming a member of a hunting organization or fraternity can be a valuable hunting tool. As most organizations circulate educational print or e-magazines, members often trade tips and strategies in these publications. Belonging to a hunting organization can also bring purpose to hunting and motivate individuals to get involved to protect the sport and challenge themselves afield. Clubs like Whitetail SLAM offer neat advantages to network with fellow, like-minded members. Whitetail SLAM offers a free hunt swap classified advertisement section on their website that gives members the opportunity to offer up trail camera photos of deer in their areas, and a chance to trade hunts with other members. Whitetail SLAM also conducts several free hunt giveaways each year, and weekly gear giveaways for members.

SCI and GSCO conduct yearly conventions that give members an opportunity to receive hunting awards and personal recognition at dinnerv banquets and parties. These gatherings include raffles, auctions and often many outfitters selling hunting opportunities. There is no better place to meet other hunters and learn about new hunting opportunities than these types of conventions.

As a final note, getting involved with hunting organizations helps hunters to carry on their hunting heritage and legacy. Documenting your slams and recording animals in the record books allows hunters to have a lasting record of their hunting accomplishments. These awards are passed down through generations of family members and offer a record of the hunter's commitment to the sport and to wildlife conservation.

More information is available at these website links:

http://www.whitetailslam.com/
http://www.wildsheep.org/
http://member.scifirstforhunters.org/
http://www.superslam.org/
http://www.pope-young.org/
http://www.nwtf.org/
http://www.boone-crockett.org/

CHAPTER 3

A DO-IT-YOURSELF SLAM

By nature, many of the recognized SLAMs exclude the do-it-yourself hunter from completion. Consider the North American Super Slam or the Grand Slam of sheep and you'll understand. This is one of the reasons that the Wild Turkey Grand Slam is so appealing to such a broad audience, simply because it's possible to bag all of the subspecies of turkeys on your own.

Although it may seem daunting, achieving the Whitetail SLAM on your own is possible as well. It's an endeavor worthy of any whitetail junkie worth his or her salt in the woods. To take four bucks from the different regions without enlisting guides, outfitters or pay-to-play operations is an achievement worthy of a little chest-puffing, especially if a few of those deer happen to come from public land. Take a DIY buck from all eight regions for your Ultimate Whitetail SLAM and you can rest easy knowing you're breathing the rarified air that only fills the lungs of the best of the best deer hunters.

Of course, unlike some of the other SLAMs available, the Whitetail SLAM also offers blue-collar hunters a chance to compete with well-heeled hunters. This is one of the best things about whitetails throughout their range – deer are more available to all hunters than any other game species.

WHERE TO START

Just where you live is going to determine how you pursue a do-it-yourself Whitetail SLAM. It's easy to look at a map of the various regions that divide the subgroups, and decide to hunt an area that offers a shot at two or

REALTREE
KILL

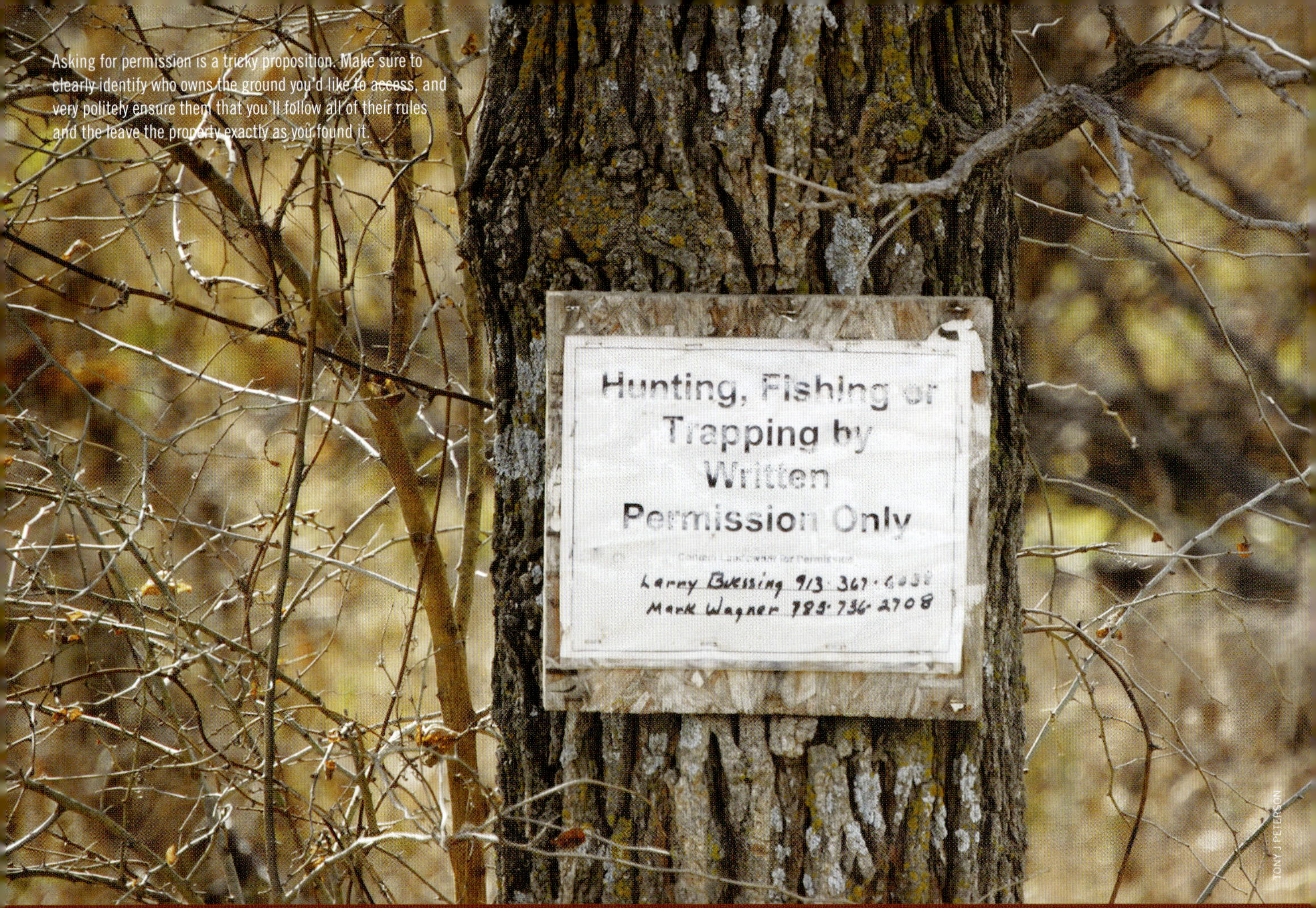

Asking for permission is a tricky proposition. Make sure to clearly identify who owns the ground you'd like to access, and very politely ensure them that you'll follow all of their rules and the leave the property exactly as you found it.

TONY J PETERSON

GAINING PRIVATE ACCESS

While many whitetailers are content to hunt public ground, television host and outdoor personality Melissa Bachman will try hard to gain access to private land when traveling to hunt. She has a few tricks up her sleeve that anyone can employ – should they glass a prime alfalfa field in a creek-bottom or spy a distant patch of hardwoods that should be teeming with deer.

"The first thing I look for is concentrations of deer before I ever ask for permission. Many times that consists of a spot that doesn't or can't be hunted, like state or federal parks. I want to find some kind of refuge of some sort, and then I'll consult my plat book. At that point it's a matter of digging a little deeper to find neighboring landowners and then knocking on their doors."

Hunters familiar with this tactic in the Midwest and the East might be in for a shock should they travel west because of the prevalence of absentee landowners and those that own huge tracts of land. Don't be discouraged if you have to sleuth a bit more to figure out just where the landowner resides, because the extra work might discourage others and lead to a quality hunting opportunity.

"Another trick I use to find hunting spots, whether they border a refuge or not, is to simply network. If I've identified an area I want to hunt, I typically show up a few days early and will pay special attention to cafe or gas station conversations. My father has the gift of gab, and I learned from him that it never hurts to strike up a conversation. Even if the stranger you start to talk to doesn't own an acre, they may know a rancher willing to let you hunt. The key is to come off as an average person, not some trophy-obsessed hunter.

"Once I get lucky and find a landowner willing to chat, I always let them know that I won't drive on their properties, even with a four-wheeler. I want to be as low impact as possible and let them know that I know they are doing me a huge favor."

No matter what type of private ground you're allowed on, if it's owned by someone else, it is a good idea to show gratification. It's a simple act that is always appreciated and may just solidify a relationship with a landowner for years.

more different deer during the same trip. While possible, this may not be the best option.

For starters, killing a single buck on any trip is no small feat, and introducing the possibility of hunting two distinct areas for two deer can muddy the waters and detract from the process as a whole. In many cases it's better to pick one region and focus on it first. For most, this will be the neighboring region to their home territory.

Wherever that region may be, the most important step will involve research. At first, this means simply finding a place to hunt. There are several ways to go about this. Devout do-it-yourself hunter and bow-hunting writer Tony Peterson starts this process by networking.

"I love to hunt public land because it's so challenging, but I won't pass up a chance to hunt private ground when available. Occasionally I'll find out someone I know has connections to private ground in an area that I'm interested in. This is a tricky situation because you never want to overstep your bounds, but if you can gain access through your connection it can be worth it. Most of the time when I'm traveling for whitetails though, I'm going to start by trying to find quality public ground."

Public land hunting has a negative connotation amongst many hunters who have been soured on the experience by low success rates and high hunting pressure. However, it's a disservice to yourself to write off all public ground because of some bad experiences.

Peterson knows this all too well. "I grew up bow-hunting public land in southeastern Minnesota with my father and we were always bumping into fellow bow-hunters and small-game hunters. It made the hunting tough, however I've found that experience doesn't exist everywhere I travel. In fact, some of the best hunting I've got occurs on public land that I found through extensive research and scouting."

To find quality public hunting land, Peterson starts by deciding on a region he wants to hunt and then taps into several resources to eliminate certain properties. "The first thing I do is order a fish and wildlife map, or a state map of the area I want to hunt. I also take a look at the state game agency's website, many of which have

HUNTER BIO | MELISSA BACHMAN

MELISSA BACHMAN

AGE/HOMETOWN:
28/Paynesville, Minn.

YEARS HUNTING: 16 Years

FAVORITE HUNT LOCATION:
West-central Illinois

DEER HARVESTED:
I'm not sure how many deer I have killed but I've been very lucky to hunt whitetails all across the country, and have taken a lot of deer and some big bucks.

LARGEST BUCK: 202 inches

FAVORITE METHOD: Spot and stalk, or rattling in the river bottoms on the ground.

CONTACT INFO:
Website: www.melissabachman.com;
TV Show: *Winchester Deadly Passion*

WHITETAIL SLAM:
No, I am one buck short at this time.

Taking a long weekend in the spring to walk potential spots and look for shed antlers is a great way to familiarize yourself with a new property, and get a leg up on the hunting come fall.

TONY J PETERSON

gotten more and more user-friendly in recent years.

"What I look for is a huge piece of public ground that is literally thousands of acres. I want to be able to get away from the crowds, and the best way I've found to do that is simply to walk farther than the next guy. This only gets better on properties that restrict treestand usage and force you to pull stands each day.

"If I can't find a huge tract of land, I look for a cluster of properties in a relatively small area. If I have five or six small pieces of ground within a half-hour drive I know I can have a backup plan if I need it, which is very important. Either way, as soon as I've identified a decent looking property, I dig in by comparing my topographic maps that show public boundaries with aerial photos so I can see what the land truly holds for whitetail-friendly areas."

Peterson's point of consulting maps and aerial photos is backed by nearly all of the top whitetail hunters in the country. It's crucial to hitting the ground running, especially during trips where time is limited. Identifying potential access points, bedding areas, food sources and travel routes well ahead of time will pay off dividends when you actually set foot on the ground.

HUNTING TIP:
SPRING SHEDS & SCOUTING

Dedicating the majority of your free time to fall hunts is nothing new to most serious whitetailers, but there is a way to spread out time away from home and still come ever closer to whitetail success. The secret is to make shed hunting and scouting forays in the springtime. Combine a trip with a turkey hunt if you have to, but any time spent looking over distant hunting spots with boots on the ground will help come fall. Every antler picked up, every scrape logged away in the memory bank, and each funnel you identify will lead you one step closer to scoring while on the road.

TIMING

When deciding to forgo outfitters and guides in search of your SLAM, the calendar is going to become either your best friend or worst enemy. Time and timing are everything, and planning when to travel may seem as

HUNTER BIO TONY PETERSON

TONY J PETERSON

AGE/HOMETOWN: 33/Andover, Minn.

YEARS HUNTING: 22 Years

FAVORITE HUNT LOCATION:
Southeastern Minnesota

DEER HARVESTED: 60-plus

LARGEST BUCK: 146 inches, 205 pounds.

FAVORITE METHOD:
Any kind of bowhunting, but I especially love DIY hunts.

CONTACT INFO:
www.tjpoutdoors.com

WHITETAIL SLAM:
I have a ¾ DIY archery SLAM.

Huntress Melissa Bachman with a great Missouri bow buck. Melissa is a talented cinematographer, television producer and the "real deal" when it comes to DIY big-game bowhunting.

MELISSA BACHMAN

TONY J PETERSON

Research is extremely important for the do-it-yourselfer looking to finish a SLAM. Aerial photos of public or private ground provide a good chance to partially learn a property before ever setting foot on it.

simple as researching peak rut dates and hitting the road for those dates. Unfortunately not everyone can drop what they're doing and hunt during peak rut dates, especially when they're hundreds of miles from home.

To figure out when to hunt, consider the region you are going to travel to. Certainly much of the South Central Plains, Northern Woodlands and Dakota regions will all feature a very similarly timed rut, and it's always a good idea to be in a tree during November in those areas. That doesn't mean September, October, or even December and January won't provide opportunities at bucks.

Colorado resident and bowhunting writer Jace Bauserman knows all about traveling outside of the prime time to try and arrow whitetails. His DIY hunts all start with plenty of planning, and he takes into account not only the timing of his hunts, but the amount of time he has available to hunt. "Oftentimes outside of the rut I'm looking for an early season hunt that fits in between chasing elk and antelope at home. If I'm going to hunt in a state close to Colorado, I look for something few others do – and that's a piece of public ground with very few trees. Trees mean treestand hunt-

TONY J PETERSON

HUNTING TIP:
THINK OUTSIDE-OF-THE-BOX

A lot of hunters shun deer drives, which is understandable. However, that doesn't mean they can't be productive, and a lot of fun to boot! Some situations are highly conducive to deer drives, like areas dotted with small woodlots. In this scenario a hunter can set up in one of the woodlots while drivers slowly make their way through nearby woodlots. The deer will run from cover to cover and should offer a high odds shot to the stander. In other situations large rivers, railroad beds and other barriers that won't stop a fleeing deer – but might influence the movement of a gently nudged deer – can be used to guide deer in a stander's direction. Even though it seems strange, during most deer drives wind direction is everything. Passing far upwind of where you presume the deer to be located is a good way to let them catch your scent without blowing them full-tilt out of the cover. The object is to get them on their feet and walking away. These types of drives can save the traveling hunter – and put a good buck in front of your sights when all other hunting methods fall short.

ing, and it seems a lot of hunters skip land that doesn't offer suitable stand trees.

"Since I'm hunting public ground, a lack of trees and an early-season hunt usually means that I'll have the property to myself. This is key because I've learned over the years to have patience, no matter whether I've got two days or 10 to hunt. I know that I only need to find one good spot to build a ground blind, or see one buck screw up and bed in a place I can stalk him. It may take a couple of days of hanging back and glassing to identify the right situations, but once I find it my odds of tagging out go way up. This is so hard to do on limited time, but is crucial especially in early-season and even late-season hunts when you can't count on the rut to push bucks past you throughout the day."

Bauserman's method of seeking out treeless, and thus less desirable properties, can work for anyone, anywhere. Just as having to work hard to get to a spot keeps competition out, many hunters simply don't see the value in certain ground. While some land is absolutely dead and not conducive to holding whitetails, it's important to remember how adaptable deer are and how good they are at avoiding us.

Savvy hunters have dialed in this mentality and it almost always sets in because of experience. Think

A good topographic map will show the division between public and private ground and tip you off to potential access sites. No hunter should hit the road on a do-it-yourself adventure without good maps.

TONY J PETERSON

It's difficult to sacrifice hunting time to scout, but patience is a virtue for a reason. Time spent learning deer patterns and identifying potential ambush sites is always well spent.

about how often you've blood-trailed a deer into an overlooked thicket or overgrown homestead only to realize it's covered in big buck rubs and scrapes. Or the random monster buck that springs from his bed in a fence line connecting woodlots. The examples could go on, but the point is that deer, especially mature bucks, tend to seek out the areas with the least amount of human intrusion – and that doesn't necessarily mean a nonhunting refuge or a part of a property that is four miles from the nearest road. It simply means that some places are ignored by hunters and at the very least, deserve a quick walk-through. Deer leave plenty of sign, and if you've decided to scratch an itch and satisfy your curiosity about a three-acre plum thicket in the middle of an agricultural field, you'll know quickly whether it's a honey-hole or a dud. Either way, it's much better to know than to wonder.

HUNT TO YOUR STRENGTHS

A lot of traveling hunters think they are going to have to reinvent the wheel when they head to a new region. This often leads them to engage in tactics they aren't familiar with or have no confidence in, both of which are bad. Occasionally, traveling from a heavily-pressured state to lightly-pressured state can cause a hunter to get sloppy as well, another negative in the whitetail woods.

Peterson has plenty of experience with these issues. "When I first started leaving my home state of Minnesota to hunt, I started in North Dakota on public land. What I couldn't believe was the amount of deer I saw and that caused me to think I could kill a good buck easily. After trying to still-hunt or stalk some whitetails I realized that simply wouldn't cut it and began to truly evaluate my ambush sites and start to hang stands, just like I do at home.

"Once I started hunting like I should, I started kill-

A lot of hunters look at traveling hunting, especially on public land, as a losing proposition. The best hunters know better though, and they also know that it's necessary to outwork the competition to end up successful.

ing more bucks. I've carried that mentality on every whitetail hunt I've gone on, and it really boils down to admitting that even in a good place I'm going to have to work hard. For me, it's all about scouting a near-perfect treestand site or ground blind and then hunting it during the right conditions. I don't call a lot or decoy much simply because I spend a lot of time chasing pressured deer, so I rely heavily on figuring out natural deer travel routes and getting in there with the wind in my face. It sounds simple, and can be, but it requires some effort to get it right."

TONY J PETERSON

GREG MILLER

Keeping your chin up on a tough hunt can be difficult, but that is one of Greg Miller's keys to success while hunting far from home. Hunters who let a negative attitude creep in and settle are sure to fail.

ATTITUDE IS EVERYTHING

When it's reduced to half-hour television shows, hunting seems too easy. That's the beauty of editing and although it makes for good entertainment, the reality is that behind even a short, guided hunt there is still a lot of time and effort put in by someone, or multiple people. This is something worth remembering when you're heading out on your own to tag a buck in a new area. It's not going to be easy, or even close to easy.

Recognizing the difficulty and keeping your head up through deerless sits or while getting busted on stand, is a tough task especially if you start tallying up the money you've spent and vacation days you've burned to not kill a buck. If there is a hunter out there who knows all about the mental aspect, it's whitetail guru and television host Greg Miller. Having traveled all over the country in search of whitetails has taught Miller to keep a tight leash on his emotions and his reality in check.

"When you travel to hunt it can be hard to stay focused. Oftentimes you're not sleeping too well, you're not eating like you should, and it just becomes tough to keep a positive outlook. I learned this years ago when I was working construction and would only get a day or two off to hunt. I took it personally if something went wrong and I wasn't successful. At one point I had a buddy call me out on it and say that it's only hunting and that I shouldn't be so negative. It was an eye-opener for me and I try really hard to not get a bad attitude no matter what happens with the weather, the deer behavior, my gear or whatever. Some things are out of your hands, your outlook isn't. This isn't to say I'm a Zen master or anything because I can still get bummed. But now, as opposed to 10 or 20 years ago, I know that I need to get over it and move on. That's important."

In the whitetail world we are collectively obsessed with tactics and go-to gear, but rarely admit to the

Tony Peterson (left) is shown here with his hunting partner, Ryan Hawkins, on a public land hunt in Nebraska. Finding a trusted partner for do-it-yourself hunts will cut down on cost and labor, and increase the chances of figuring the deer out on a short hunt.

TONY J PETERSON

power of attitude. It's not some new-age philosophy, just a simple acknowledgement of the reality of staying positive – and how that can carry through to the last few minutes of shooting light, when all of the negatives can disappear at the sound of shuffling hooves in the leaf litter.

PARTNER UP

Even though we all have hunting buddies, someone that is a good traveling hunting partner is a different breed. Camp chores, competition over good spots, and a willingness to pay their share all can make or break a good hunting partner. This is why some of the best hunters travel alone, but that doesn't mean it's necessary to go solo. In fact, a trusted partner can make hunting much easier.

For starters, the scouting portion of any DIY hunt becomes less difficult with a divide-and-conquer strategy. Two or more hunters glassing different fields or scouring distant bedding areas through spotting scopes will learn more than an individual ever could. An extra set of eyes is important, but so is having an extra set of hands to help hang stands and trim shooting lanes. All of the work associated with hunting whitetails correctly can be made easier with a little help.

When it comes to the hunting, setting up in two different spots will provide twice the opportunities to observe deer and get them dialed in. Of course, should an arrow or bullet fly true, then having help is always appreciated. As is having someone to shoulder the financial burden of driving long distances and living off of road food for a hunt. Don't shy away from hitting the road with a buddy; just make sure they are the right fit for your goals and hunting styles.

A do-it-yourself SLAM might seem out of reach, but it's not. Depending on individual location and willingness to put some miles on your hunting truck, ending up in new regions with freshly-minted tags in your pocket is a real possibility. Many hunters shy away from this style because it can seem daunting to conduct research, scout and hunt unfamiliar ground. However, if you devote some time to research and scouting long before the season opens, and then hunt to your strengths – you may find that an extremely rewarding SLAM is within your grasp.

CHAPTER 4

NORTHERN WOODLANDS

(Odocoileus virginianus borealis)

Easily one of the most diverse regions of the Whitetail SLAM, the Northern Woodlands region covers territory ranging from heavy agriculture to endless miles of deeply-wooded mountains. Due to this diversity, whitetail hunters in this region may employ wildly different tactics to tag their buck, which will depend largely on the locality they plan to hunt.

For instance, if you take to the field in the southwestern corner of this region, typical field-hunting tactics will come into play. Travel farther north though, and it will be time to up your sign-interpretation game. Head east to the seaboard and you'll have to pay close attention to scent control and hunting pressure because in most situations you'll have plenty of hunting competition. Travel north from there and you'll start to get into mountainous terrain that is going to require serious research and boots on the ground to figure out just where a buck might live, let alone how to kill him. You are just as likely to find a smoking fresh rub line leading across an old beaver dam in the back of a cranberry bog as you are a community scrape underneath a white oak tree in this region, and that diversity certainly contributes to the beauty of chasing whitetails in the Northern Woodlands region.

Of course, this is the beauty of whitetail hunting anywhere...

EMBRACING TECHNOLOGY

One individual who has not only made a well-respected name for himself in the arena of all-things-deer, but has also taken his share of Northern Woodlands bucks is Bill Winke. Through his years of outdoors writing and more recently his dedication to producing quality television, like his educational and entertaining Midwest Whitetail show, Winke's name has become synonymous with taking a systematic and intelligent approach to targeting and outsmarting bucks. Over the

JOHN HAFNER

Northern Woodlands whitetails are the most pursued of all the subgroups.

ALL ABOUT THE NORTHERN WOODLANDS DEER

BY DR. HARRY JACOBSON

RANGE

The Northern Woodlands' range encompasses diverse habitat over an expansive area from central to eastern Canada, south throughout Minnesota, Wisconsin and Illinois, then east through Indiana, Michigan, Ohio, Pennsylvania and New York. Maryland marks the southern edge of the borealis' range along the Atlantic seaboard, and the northerly reaches extend up through Maine and Nova Scotia.

These lands were once covered by mature forest, with few deer present. But logging, agriculture and other activities of settlement resulted in a boon for the deer with the creation of habitat capable of sustaining great numbers of deer. Through the educational efforts of groups like QDMA and many other conservation organizations, as well as local hunter cooperatives, Northern Woodlands whitetail herds have never been in better shape.

RUT TIMING

Breeding begins as the amount of daylight shortens in late October into December, with its peak in mid-November, a magical time when all deer hunters abandon most thoughts and activities in favor of being in the woods. Bucks become very susceptible to calling and rattling from Halloween through the first week in November as they get on their feet in search of does.

PHYSICAL CHARACTERISTICS

Cold-weather-adapted, massive-bodied animals are the norm in Northern reaches of the range. Good, quality habitat grows mature bucks with body sizes in excess of 300 pounds and antlers that can grow well beyond the minimum scores required for entry in the Boone and Crockett, or Pope and Young record books. Deer follow "Bergmann's rule," a well-known law of biology that states body size increases as you travel north because large bodies are more energy efficient in cold climates, and vice versa. Hunters are often amazed at the size differences as they move even one state north or south. Although body size generally increases as you travel north, the most fertile soils and croplands generally produce the highest average antler measurements.

years Winke has been there and done it all to kill whitetails, and his current go-to strategy is one that most hunters can utilize provided they pay close attention to the details.

"Something that I'm doing is truly gathering information from our trail cameras. We've figured out which bucks to hunt and how to hunt them from the information we've gleaned from our cameras. In fact, we come really close to killing every buck that we go after now, which is pretty cool when you're trying to kill a single buck on purpose," Winke explained when asked of his current hunting secrets.

"To start this strategy it's important to identify a food source. For me, in many places that is either a small agricultural field or a food plot. In the big woods that may be a clearcut of the right age or even a few early-dropping oak trees on a ridge. What I like to do is set up a camera on a hot food source and run it for about 10 days or so. That has proven to be long enough to get most deer on camera, and will often let you identify which bucks are going to make your

TO LEASE OR NOT TO LEASE

Owner of outdoors-related media company Theory 13 Creative, Tim Kent, decided to take matters into his own hands after years of bumping into other hunters while hunting in New York and New Jersey. "We were simply tired of having people on top of us, especially in my home state of New York, so I got together with my father and two hunting buddies and decided to lease some ground.

"I ran an advertisement in the local penny saver with the headline, 'Landowners - Want Some Help Paying Your Taxes?' The response was overwhelming and it allowed me to walk lots of different properties to see what would work best. Some of the landowners only wanted a couple of dollars per acre, while others were asking upwards of $30. We settled in the middle on a 370-acre property. Since then, we've included other land and now have 620 acres to hunt. Originally I didn't want to lease, but it has been the best thing for my hunting."

Kent's experience certainly mirrors whitetail hunters across the country, not just in the Northeast. Investigating lease options might lead to a long-term solution to finding and keeping access to hunting ground.

TIM KENT

New York state hunter Tim Kent decided to find some ground to lease after years of bumping into other hunters in his area. The decision has paid dividends each fall since.

Well-known *Dominant Bucks* hunter Joel Snow shows off the awesome genetics of central Ohio with this 200-inch monster.

JOEL SNOW

hit list. If possible, dumping corn or other attractants in front of your camera can be a shortcut to identifying all of the bucks in your hunting area."

No matter how you decide to approach this initial stage, make sure it occurs after the bucks are established in their fall patterns. Although it's extremely popular to run cameras in the summer to catch images of velvet-antlered bucks, the information you can glean from such images only goes so far considering some of those bucks will disperse to new areas once they shed their velvet.

To further break down the first stage Winke advises, "This quick-inventory period lets you identify all, or nearly all of the local bucks. Take special note of which direction the deer approach from and if any of the target bucks are showing up during daylight. If they are coming from a certain area where there might be a creek crossing, a ditch crossing, or some other pinch point, I might move a camera to that spot to see if I can get an earlier-in-the-day picture and further peg down an individual buck's movements. From this stage alone I gather a lot of background information on the deer I want to target.

BILL WINKE

This buck, nicknamed Loppy, was at least 7½ years old when Bill Winke killed him. Employing a year-to-year trail camera strategy paid off on this reclusive deer.

"This strategy works great in agricultural areas because it's much easier to pin down food sources. If you're in the big woods of Wisconsin, Michigan, the northeast or even Canada, you'll need to run more cameras to just identify the right spots to take inventory. From that point, it's a matter of moving the camera to pin down an exact corner or trail that your target deer is using. For us, that's always a mature deer because of what we like to hunt, but for many hunters that might just be a buck of any size. Either way, it's necessary to try to figure out which deer are showing up in daylight and therefore killable. Many times I'll run my cameras on a time-lapse mode to cover more areas and show me only the bucks that are moving during shooting hours.

"Eventually, by studying the trail camera images you'll start to learn individual preferences and that bucks have their own personalities. These reveal clues to just how you can set up and kill a particular deer if you know what to look for. Again, this takes time so it's not possible for everyone, but will work if you're just in it to tag out on any buck. No matter what kind of deer you're targeting, you need to be careful about checking your cameras and alerting the deer to your presence. I wear waders in to check my cameras whenever possible so that I don't leave any scent."

TONY J PETERSON

Young bucks like this northern Wisconsin six-pointer might not be your target deer, or they just might. According to noted whitetail hunter and author Bill Winke, trail cameras are one of the best tools at your disposal for pinning down exact daylight movements of specific deer.

This point is something that anyone who relies on trail cameras should understand very clearly. Although cameras are a near-perfect tool for acquiring knowledge, they can also represent a double-edged sword when it comes to frequency of visits to a certain area, and too much reliance on them. This is especially true

HUNTER BIO | BILL WINKE

BILL WINKE

AGE/HOMETOWN: 49/Waukon, Iowa

YEARS HUNTING: 36 years

FAVORITE HUNT LOCATION: Iowa (my home ground)

DEER HARVESTED: Hundreds

LARGEST BUCK: 206 inches gross, 260 pounds.

FAVORITE METHOD: Bowhunting

CONTACT INFO: www.midwestwhitetail.com, *Midwest Whitetail TV* on The Sportsman Channel.

WHITETAIL SLAM: I am sure I have at least a partial slam, but don't have one registered.

Minnesota huntress Melissa Bachman shows off some dynamite antler sheds.

in areas with high hunting pressure, where the deer that you're targeting can be put down by small-game hunters, bird watchers or other deer hunters all using the same ground as you. Although you can't control intrusion from others, you can control the amount of pressure you put on certain deer. It may sound strange but this is one advantage weekend hunters have, because due to life's obligations they are forced to give their spots a five-day break every week. This can be the perfect scenario to letting a camera, or multiple cameras, do the work for you while you're gone.

Along those same lines Winke brought up an interesting point about his trail camera strategy, "I always try to match the human presence in my area. If I'm hunting an agricultural area, that means using a truck or four-wheeler to get to my cameras when possible. This is simply because that's how a farmer would go into his field and those actions aren't viewed as negative by the deer. In the big woods, it's time to up your game further and pay close attention to scent control, the noise you make, and the direction you enter and exit. This is because a big buck in a swamp or other roadless wilderness is not likely to run into a human that is not hunting him.

"After all of this, I only hunt the right conditions. This may seem like a lot of work, but it's the fun part of deer hunting and I've found it's extremely rewarding to identify a buck, peg him down, and eventually arrow

Ohio buck hunter Adam Hays has taken three 200-inch whitetails with a bow as well as a Whitetail SLAM.

him." Winke's strategy requires two things that are the cornerstones of any good whitetail hunter – discipline and patience. To keep up with scent control day in and day out, hunt only when Mother Nature gives you a break, and wait for the deer that you've got your heart set on, is no easy task. Then again, consistently killing whitetails anywhere is rarely easy, but always rewarding.

LESS IS MORE

Winke's strategy is perfect for hunters who have a setup with controlled access and can afford multiple cameras. Some hunters may find themselves in a different situation but still wish to pin down deer via cameras. Bowhunting writer, Tony Peterson, looks at cameras a bit differently.

"Since I hunt a lot of public land, and even private land with other hunters, I use my cameras sparingly. This is because I really want to minimize the amount of time I go into certain areas and simply because my cameras have a tendency to disappear from time to time.

"So I tend to use them to answer a specific question I might have. For example, if I've been scouting heavily, either on the ground or via maps and aerial

ADAM HAYS

photos, I may rely on a camera to cover a tiny waterhole or a single river crossing that has caught my attention. I typically use a trail camera mount and a few tree steps to hang my cameras about nine or 10 feet off of the ground. This gives me the chance to avoid theft and offers a better angle for pictures. I just want to get a quick glimpse of what deer are going through a spot and whether I think I can set a stand there, or reverse engineer their travel a little bit to catch them somewhere else. A lot of times this serves to scratch a potential stand site off of my list so I can move on to other areas."

DEATH-CURL CALLING

New York bowhunter and deer calling expert Cy Weichert has taken a pile of Northern Woodlands bucks via deer calling, although he employs a different strategy than most. "I have been calling bucks into bow range for the past 30 years, and have perfected the art of mouth calling to the point where I don't believe there is a buck out there that I can't get to come to my calls!"

Confidence like that comes from serious success, and although most hunters think it's simply a matter of making the right sounds, that's only a small portion of what goes into calling in a buck to kill him. "I'd argue that calling in a buck to bow-kill involves a 10/90 percent split between making the right calls and setting up in a position that will allow you to kill him once he responds. I call it the 'death curl,' but what it really means is that most bucks, especially mature bucks, will trust their noses more than anything when they approach your calling location. This means they'll almost always curl downwind, which is where I'll be ready to shoot them in a carefully planned-out shooting lane. In the past seven seasons I've harvested five mature bucks, all of which circled downwind at 25 to 30 yards – right into my shooting lanes."

Weichert's strategy of combining calling with setup considerations is the hallmark of a hunter who understands deer behavior and how to use it against them.

CY WEICHERT

Mouth-calling expert Cy Weichert uses a buck's tendency to curl downwind in his favor when calling. Knowing that a mature deer is most likely to circle downwind allows Weichert the chance to plan for a buck's approach, and get ready to arrow him as he responds to the calling.

Peterson's last point is worthy of some consideration. If you've done everything right as far as scent control and approach to your camera site, you should know what's going on in the area. If that knowledge happens to be that the deer aren't using it frequently or they are only using it at night, don't belabor the spot. Move on to new areas and keep hunting, as opposed to waiting for something to happen in a dead area.

Also, it's important to realize that some places just aren't conducive to high-odds hunting despite the fact that you might get great pictures. Depending on wind direction and other conditions, bucks might travel through like they own the place. That's because they do, and because they've got their nose, ears and eyes working for them in a situation that offers them a much better advantage than you. Recognizing those situations and how to adapt is the key to hunting big bucks, especially in areas of heavy hunting pressure.

In this aerial photo you can see two potential stand sites that are ideal for decoying whitetails. This "hourglass" setup is one of the situations Stan Potts looks for while researching new properties. Due to the shape of the field and opposing points of woods, most cruising bucks will choose to cross between the points. This puts them in a perfect position to spot a decoy, and allows for two stand sites that will cover a wide variety of potential wind directions.

A VIEW FROM ABOVE

The core premise of the Whitetail SLAM is to travel in search of whitetail hunting opportunities, and to prove that you've got the chops to successfully harvest whitetail bucks in vastly different areas. One such hunter, who has more than proven he has the goods to make it happen, is Stan Potts. Potts has taken more 200-class bucks than most hunters have ever laid eyes on, and is the host of *North American Whitetail TV*.

When asked about how he would go about hunting a new spot in the Northern Woodlands region, he had plenty of things to say and they all involved a common theme, which is research.

"If I'm heading to this region to hunt, the first thing I rely on is aerial photos of the exact area I'm going to hunt. I don't like to go any place without an aerial photo that I can sit down with and thoroughly study. I want to use that photo to break down the entire area and identify hardwood ridges, agriculture, creek bottoms, food sources, clearcuts, anything that might give me an advantage when I actually get on the ground. After identifying basic whitetail-friendly areas, I'll take it a step further and try to find pinch points and funnels.

"Since the majority of time I spend in the Northern Woodlands region occurs during the late pre-rut through the late rut, I'm also looking for very specific treestand sites while pouring over my aerial photos. In addition to looking for obvious travel corridors, I'm also looking for different shades in the timber on my aerial photos. If you learn what to look for you might just see an old fenceline running through a woodlot, or you might see the difference between an old clearcut and a fresh one. You can also see the difference between

TONY J PETERSON

According to deer hunting guru Stan Potts, if you're going to travel to the Northern Woodlands Region to hunt whitetails, you better study up on aerial photography so that you can hit the ground running once your hunt starts.

hardwoods and thickets. I take into account all of these terrain features when deciding on where I might want to hang a stand."

Finding likely stand sites and how to hunt them via aerial photos takes time but is well worth it. Food sources – especially agricultural fields – are easy enough to identify, but the subtle fencelines, delineation between new growth and old growth, and a quality pinch point versus a poor funnel are also evident if you know what to look for. So how do you know? For starters, take a property that you've hunted for a long time and look at it on Google Earth or another aerial photo website. What exactly does your favorite ridge look like? Or that old overgrown homestead? Ask yourself what your favorite stand sites look like from a satellite's view. This information can travel with you as you scout new spots that might be hundreds of miles from your home territory.

BACK TO EARTH

Potts is a decoy-hunting junkie and is always on the lookout for situations where he can pop out a faux buck and await a live challenger. "I'm always looking

KIP ADAMS

According to cementum annuli aging, this Pennsylvania buck was 8½ years old when Wildlife Biologist Kip Adams (pictured with his daughter) shot him. High hunter densities in the area typically prevent bucks from reaching half of that age, which makes it a truly special trophy.

HUNTER BIO | STAN POTTS

STAN POTTS

AGE/HOMETOWN: 62/Clinton, Ill.

YEARS HUNTING: Since 1965

FAVORITE HUNT LOCATION:
Illinois (home state), Iowa, Ohio, Kansas.

DEER HARVESTED:
50–100 P&Y, hundreds of deer total.

LARGEST BUCK:
220 inches gross nontypical, over 230 pounds.

FAVORITE METHOD:
Decoys, rattling and calling.

CONTACT INFO:
www.huntthemidwest.com
www.dominantbucks.com

WHITETAIL SLAM: Yes

Stan Potts poses with his four 200-inch whitetails. In 2012 Stan shot another buck in the 190s, which would have given him five 200-inch bucks.

NORTHERN WOODLANDS HUNTING TIPS

I used to believe that bucks moved into and out of my hunting area during the rut all of the time. After extensive trail camera usage, I've realized that is not true. While it does happen, you're far more likely to simply catch a daylight glimpse of a buck that has been there all along instead of a new deer cruising through. If you've been on a largely nocturnal deer, knowing this can help you kill him because in reality, there are far fewer rut surprises than originally thought. - *Bill Winke*

If you're scanning aerial photos of your hunting grounds pay particular attention to creeks and smaller rivers. A bend in those waterways will usually feature a shallow area downstream, which might turn out to be a key deer crossing. Not all of them will be conducive to treestands due to terrain and wind, but they are worth checking out, especially during periods of intense rutting activity. - *Stan Potts*

for my ideal decoying situation. This consists of a field or clearcut that has got timber on both sides and forms a sort of hourglass shape with opposing points on both sides. This represents the best spot for a buck to cross and will almost always be the most ideal location to find the perfect setup. In addition to being a high-odds spot for cruising bucks, this also gives me the opportunity to set up stands on both sides to hunt multiple wind directions. Having options like that is extremely important when you're on a travel hunt.

"Naturally, all of this aerial photo study is important, however it doesn't mean much until you actually sneak into a spot. When I show up at the place I'm going to hunt I'll be very careful and just do a quick on-the-ground scouting session in each of the areas that have caught my interest. From there, I'll hang stands for specific winds and get ready to hunt, although my work still isn't finished because I know that I might need to tweak my spot after I've hunted. I'm a big proponent of the fact that if you're moving, you are killing. So, if I see a buck cruise by out of range one morning, I'll wait until midday and move my setup to exactly where he travelled to try to kill him on the very next sit."

Potts' strategy for heavy research is something every whitetail hunter should take to heart, especially if you plan to travel in search of your Whitetail SLAM. The value of the pre-hunt research cannot be overstated, and it will prove its worth once you show up in your new hunting spot. His point of validating his aerial research by walking the hunting ground cannot be overstated either. Aerial photography can provide a great foundation for a successful hunt, but that doesn't mean the building is complete. Boots on the ground cannot be beat, and carefully investigating a milk run of potential stand sites will pull all of the pieces together and tell you not only where to set up, but where not to.

A VARIED REGION

Certified Wildlife Biologist Kip Adams is extremely familiar with the Northern Woodland region. "This subgroup is one of my favorites thanks in part to my time spent as the Deer & Bear Biologist with the New Hampshire Fish & Game Department. These deer have huge body weights and impressive antler potential. We've seen legitimate, certified weights of 300 pounds on some of the bucks that have come out of this region, which is reason enough to hunt them!

"If you plan to hunt this region you'll quickly realize it's all about densities – deer and hunter. Some of the states like Pennsylvania have high hunter densities, but may also have high deer densities. Others, especially as you travel farther north, will feature lower densities of

TONY J PETERSON

To tag out in the Northern Woodlands region, you'll need to hunt smart and hard. Cutting corners on any aspect of the hunt could cost you, especially if you hunt farther north where deer densities are thinner and the hunting is tougher.

TONY J PETERSON

In areas with little to no agriculture, it's a good idea to study up on regional botany to identify some of the food sources deer are likely to key on.

ISTOCK

In many areas of the Northern Woodlands region, you might find yourself hunting in the snow by the time peak rut hits. Hunters in the Northeast still use heavy snowfall to their advantage by taking to a fresh buck track and following him until they catch up to him, or jump the buck from his bed.

both deer and hunters.

"Throughout the region, hunters will also encounter varying land ownership obstacles. While much of the region is privately-owned and difficult to access, there are also a lot of public hunting opportunities starting in northern Wisconsin and stretching throughout the region in the New England states like New Hampshire's White Mountain National Forest or New York's Adirondack National Forest.

"No matter where you plan to hunt in the Northern Woodland region, it's necessary to become at the very least an amateur botanist. Deer can eat over 600 species of plants and forage and you just might find yourself hunting deer that are munching on soft-mast like apples, hackberries, dewberries, or hard-mast like acorns and beechnuts.

"Identifying these types of foods might not seem that important but consider this fact: Last year in the Northern Woodland region Illinois grew 13 million acres of corn, while the entire Northeast produced only 4 million acres. Typical agriculture hunting practices will work in this region, but opportunities are very limited.

"Another limited and truly unique hunting opportunity that occurs almost exclusively in this region, though, is big woods tracking. Huge tracts of public land or paper company land that is open to the public provide the chance to get on a good buck's track and follow it until you catch him off guard or bump him from his bed. This is an old firearm's hunting strategy and is one of the toughest ways to kill a buck, and demonstrates a serious level of woodsmanship and perseverance."

If you're into big-bodied bucks, big woods, and challenging hunting then look no further than the Northern Woodlands region when planning out the next phase of your Whitetail SLAM. It's fair to expect a challenging hunt, however tagging out on a buck in this region might just prove to be your most rewarding deer of the SLAM. You'll never know until you try!

CHAPTER 5

SOUTHEASTERN REGION

(Odocoileus virginianus virginianus)

One of the smaller regions of the Whitetail SLAM, the Southeastern Region still offers highly diverse habitat and the opportunity to tag out on a bruiser. This region also offers abundant antlerless tags in many of the states, and features a high level of hunting pressure that hunters in most of the other regions will never witness. Due to the severity of hunting pressure and the methods associated with them, this is one of the toughest regions to kill a mature buck in – although there are sleeper areas like parts of Kentucky that are churning out impressive bucks each season.

Hunters traveling to the Southeastern Region with hopes of tagging a buck and edging ever closer to their SLAM will have their pick of hunting methods ranging from common tactics like food plots and baiting, to far less common tactics like hound hunting. All promise the chance for a unique experience and while this region won't cough up mature bucks as readily as some of the regions to the west, it will provide opportunities at deer. If you're not hung up on waiting for a Booner, the Southeastern Region might suit you just fine.

That is, of course, if you can find a place to hunt. As with all of the areas of the United States and southern Canada, there is public ground in this region, but private land will prove a better bet for the traveling hunter. One particular hunter that knows all of the steps to the dance that is achieving permission to hunting ground, is South Carolina resident and devout whitetailer Joe Miles.

GET IN THE DOOR

When asked about his secrets for obtaining trust from landowners and the eventual green light to hunt, Miles had plenty to say. "This may sound strange, but I try to find properties that don't allow hunting. The pressure in our area is amazing. We can use rifles, dogs, and there is no limit on bucks. This means it's really dif-

Despite popular opinion, big bucks are found in the Southeast. Often these brutes are nocturnal and living in dense cover.

ISTOCK

ALL ABOUT THE SOUTHEASTERN DEER

BY DR. HARRY JACOBSON

RANGE

These lands were some of the earliest settled areas of the U.S., and unregulated subsistence and market hunting depleted populations to devastatingly low levels. In efforts to restock populations in the early to mid-1900s, restocking programs introduced deer from many parts of the Midwest and northern states, and in the case of Mississippi, even from Mexico.

The fact that some introduced genetics might be present in these animals does not diminish the unique aspects of the Southeastern whitetail. Many view hunting Southeastern whitetails as an experience that is as captivating and memorable as any, and the opportunity for hunting is vast through over-the-counter tags, liberal bag limits and public lands.

RUT TIMING

The average breeding dates begin in the second and third weeks of November. West Virginia begins as early as November 8, and Georgia as late as December 15, with rut activity kicking into gear around Thanksgiving. In Alabama and Mississippi, breeding varies depending on specific geographic regions. Depending on the area, breeding peaks anywhere from late November through mid-January, enabling northern hunters the chance to hunt the full season close to home and then travel to these late-rut states to enjoy a second rut, and an extended season. Before scheduling your hunt check the state agency's website for information on specific rut times for the area you will be hunting.

PHYSICAL CHARACTERISTICS

Generally, the Southeastern whitetail is a medium-sized deer with an average buck standing 40 inches high at the shoulder and weighing from 120 to more than 200 pounds. Size can vary greatly, and the deer generally get smaller as habitat moves away from the agricultural areas and fertile river bottom forests, to localities with diminished food quality like mountain habitats.

ficult to tag a mature buck here, so the first thing I look for is a property that has been off-limits to hunters for years, or at the very least doesn't allow rifle hunting."

"Once I identify a property like this, I'll do anything I can to get permission to hunt it. I've paid money outright, bought tickets to NASCAR races, and done my share of manual labor to help the landowner out."

Miles' method of doing whatever it takes to get on private ground might sound over-the-top to hunters in regions with far less pressure, but he offers good advice to all. You never know when you'll lose permission to hunt ground due to property being sold, a ticked-off landowner, or a litany of unforeseeable reasons. If you find yourself without hunting ground, you might just have to help out with chores, bust out your checkbook, or fish around for a great gift idea. This can seem to cheapen the pursuit, but it's the way of the future and is not going away. Plus, it's important to remember that one of the biggest favors anyone can offer a hunter is the opportunity to hunt deer on their property, and it's a privilege not to be taken lightly.

RANDY TEMPLETON

Bowhunting from trees has been used by native tribes for over a thousand years, but the modern treestand has changed the way we hunt whitetails.

GAME ON!

Once Miles gains permission to a piece of ground, he scours the area for a long-distance scouting advantage. "I love beanfields. They offer the perfect long-distance scouting opportunity and almost always draw in mature bucks, especially if they are somewhat secluded. Once I find that situation I'll glass and try to find a mature buck that is comfortable enough to enter the field during daylight. This may seem simple enough, but we have an August 15 opener here and our deer tend to go nocturnal in a hurry."

Miles then engages in more than simply watching

HUNTER BIO | JOE MILES

JOE MILES

AGE/HOMETOWN: 38/Columbia, S.C.

YEARS HUNTING: Over 30 years

FAVORITE HUNT LOCATION:
Suburban woodlots in the Midwest.

DEER HARVESTED: Over 100

LARGEST BUCK:
187⅝ inches, 297 pounds.

FAVORITE METHOD: Bowhunting

the buck night after night through his optics, he also tries to learn about the buck. Or specifically, which conditions are conducive to that deer showing up on certain trails with shooting light left. Everyone knows that deer of all ages and sizes use the wind to their advantage, but mature bucks live off of their noses and they almost always travel with the wind in their favor, especially in the early season.

"I make notes of which wind direction makes a particular buck the most comfortable. That's the wind that I plant to hunt him during and when I've identified the prevailing direction he prefers, I wait for a midday storm or rain shower. That's when I'll drop whatever I'm doing and sneak in there with my stand and pruning tools. I want to get my stand hung and my shooting lanes cut while it's pouring rain, at least two or three weeks before I plant to hunt."

Strategies such as going in during the rain speak volumes about a hunter and their understanding of pressured bucks. Lightly-pressured deer are tolerant of mistakes, heavily-pressured deer are not. They are survival machines and they don't abide sloppy hunting tactics or an ignorance of details, and this goes not only for older bucks but does as well. A cagey doe can just as easily cost you a mature buck as easily as the buck himself, and does oftentimes do thanks to their propensity to travel to food sources earlier than their antlered counterparts.

A word of caution surrounding Miles' strategy for hanging stands and clearing brush during rainstorms – be careful. Slick tree steps, poor visibility and a host of other factors create a more dangerous situation than

States in the Southeast have the most liberal deer hunting laws and limits. This group of bachelor bucks shows that deer numbers in the South justify these rules.

simply skipping out during bluebird skies and beautiful weather to conduct your deer preparation chores. If you're dead-set on using the cover of storms, ask a buddy along. That not only ensures someone will be there to help should something go wrong, but also greatly cuts down on the work associated with cutting shooting lanes and setting stands. As always – wear your safety harness from the ground up.

IF AT FIRST YOU DON'T SUCCEED...

Upon the opener, Miles will sneak in to his stand once the wind is right and try to catch the target buck while it is still in the same pattern. Sometimes it works, sometimes it doesn't. "If for whatever reason I don't kill

HUNTING STRATEGY: DISTANT BAYING

Hound hunting is about as popular as an anti-gun politician in the Deep South. However, unlike the misguided politician, hound hunting has garnered a negative reputation because of a lack of understanding. Once very popular, hunting deer with hounds now exists in pockets in the Southeast and in a very limited capacity in Ontario, Canada. As with any style of hunting, it's easy to judge but unfair until you've experienced it for yourself. It's still a challenging tactic that can draw you deep into the swamp and leave you sweaty, muddy and deerless while teaching another valuable lesson about deer and their ability to escape danger. Additionally, there is a very social aspect to hound hunting that has grown ever more rare as we've collectively turned our focus to big antlers and individual success in the deer woods.

High hunting pressure in the Southeastern Region means you either pony up for a property you can control, or you fight the crowds and try to out-hunt the other guys. This will involve serious scouting and the ability to outthink not only the deer, but also your two-legged competition.

TONY J PETERSON

South Carolina hunter Joe Miles has taken his share of good bucks in the Southeastern Region. He spends much of his time scouting specific bucks and figuring out how to hunt them in a way other hunters will ignore. Miles has a registered Whitetail SLAM.

him on the first sit, I know I need to pay attention to how I exit the field." Just like other hunters across the country, Miles will arrange for someone to drive out and pick him up at dark so that he won't blow out the field and sour the spot.

Once he is safely out, he'll take a few steps backward and try to figure out what happened. "I often go back the next afternoon and glass, which is hard to do when the season is open. But I want to know if I just missed him or if he has gone nocturnal, and if I think he has done just that, I'll look for a back-up plan, which involves water sources. I'll scout for the most relevant or localized water source in the immediate area because this far south, those deer will be close to water. Even if there is a swamp or other huge source of standing water, the deer – especially the bucks – will still have their favorite water source. I want to find that, and usually do either by setting up cameras or simply looking for big tracks in the mud."

Every aspiring SLAMMER out there can learn from Miles' last statement. If what you're doing isn't working, rethink your strategy. This is key to success in many areas and an absolute must for hunters competing against other hunters for the same deer.

THE OTHER SIDE OF THE COIN

While many hunters fall squarely into the same category as Miles, others end up hunting properties like the Alabama ground that Dennis Campbell owns. Camp-

TONY J. PETERSON

HUNTING TIP:
HUNT THE OPPOSITES

Big-buck addict Joe Miles is not one to hunt in lockstep with all of his competition – in fact he often deviates from typical tactics. If everyone is sitting over bait piles or food plots, he'll seek out natural food sources like persimmons, catbriers and acorns. His goal is to find anything natural that bucks will prefer because it doesn't take them long to catch on to the hunting pressure associated with a pile of corn or a food plot. The same goes for hunting a farm with lots of agriculture. Most hunters will sit field edges, so Miles seeks out stand sites in the thicker cover where mature bucks are more likely to slip up and move during daylight.

bell, who has hunted every huntable continent and killed over 300 species of game worldwide, still counts the Southeastern whitetail as his favorite to hunt out of everything he has experienced.

"I've averaged 30 days a year whitetail hunting, with a majority of it occurring in Alabama. I absolutely love hunting the Southeastern whitetails, and get more joy from outsmarting an old buck on our property than anything else." If that statement doesn't speak to the power whitetails have over us as hunters, it's hard to understand what else could. They simply get into your blood, and Campbell's not the only well-traveled hunter to express those exact sentiments. Hunters often debate amongst themselves over which game animals are the hardest to hunt, and although many mountain-dwelling species are much harder to get to, whitetails almost always top the list or end up real close. At least mature whitetails do.

"The secret to hunting in our area is to have control of a piece of ground. That doesn't mean you're out of luck if you can't afford to buy land, because you can still get together with some hunting buddies and lease a property. Either way, controlling who sets foot on the land and just where they set their feet is extremely important, and becomes absolutely crucial if you plan to target bucks that are at least 4½ years old or older, which is the caliber of deer we are after."

This advice can be a bit divisive, however that doesn't make it untrue. Having control over a property does

Although there might be water readily available in the form of swamps or rivers in the Southeastern Region, the deer are still likely to prefer a localized source. Scouting with trail cameras or actually looking for big tracks at the water's edge will reveal the presence of a good buck.

GREGG RITZ

New Hampshire hunter Gregg Ritz arrowed this Southeastern velvet buck on the opening day of the season. Ritz has also registered his Whitetail SLAM.

make it much easier to kill mature bucks, but that doesn't mean it's easy. It also doesn't mean you have to lease or buy a large chunk of ground. But hunter-controlled land in its many forms seems to be the way of the future and it would be wise to at least acknowledge that inevitability.

PLAY IT SAFE

Campbell's secret to success in the Southeastern Region is simple. "I'd love to say that I'm a great whitetail tactician, but the reality is after hunting them for so long I rely heavily on a couple of simple rules. The first is that we create sanctuaries for the deer that no one is allowed to enter. These might be drainages, swamps or thick creek bottoms. Anything nasty and gnarly that the deer will use as a bedding area can make a good sanctuary."

Sanctuaries are often looked at as something that is man-made, or at the very least planned out by man as is the case with Campbell's property, but they exist naturally throughout the whitetail's entire range. Identifying those areas that the deer love and people overlook is one of the best ways to consistently tag mature deer. But, they require patience and the fortitude to hunt intelligently without tipping your hand to the deer that are comfortable using the sanctuary.

To maintain sanctuary status on his property Campbell and his hunting partners only scout in the spring. "Long story short, scouting needs to be done in the spring so that the intrusion will be long forgotten by the time hunting season opens. Twenty-one years ago when I got this property the deer were nocturnal. We have turned them into killable deer by regulating our pressure and focusing heavily on hunting the rut, although we do kill mature bucks fairly often in the early season as well."

GREEN FIELDS EVERYWHERE

In addition to maintaining sanctuaries throughout his hunting ground, Campbell also engages in one of the few tactics that has truly allowed us to transition from hunters to stewards of the land – food plots. "We are very good at planting green fields now. Whether they contain oats, wheat, rye, clover or whatever, we maintain our food plots and try to make them highly attractive to the local does. Then when the rut occurs we wait for the does to draw our bucks out into the fields."

Food plots are a hot-button topic amongst hunters because of the perception given by hunting television and other outdoor media. The reality is, well-heeled hunters will often put in food plots because they work and are rewarding. That doesn't preclude working class hunters though. Inexpensive, small kill plots can be planted just about anywhere with a minimum amount of tools and sweat equity. They won't draw in hordes of deer like larger plots, but they just might provide a solid chance to pattern a good-sized buck and position him for the ideal shot. This is especially true for early season bow-hunters, but can also benefit firearms hunters later in the season because just like Campbell's experiences, a tiny food plot might get claimed by a single doe group that could draw a rutting buck into range.

A CHANGING CULTURE

Quality Deer Management Associate Wildlife Biologist Kip Adams is intimately familiar with the deer of the Southeastern Region. "I love this area because of the tremendous hunting culture, part of which is the prevalence of hunting clubs. There is a lot of timber company land in this region and much of it is leased by hunting clubs. Hunters in the Southeast have a unique opportunity to join a hunting club and become a part of that tradition."

That tradition includes the hunting clubs, but also a culture that is slowly recognizing the potential for quality deer management. "We used to think that the North had most of the big deer and that the South simply had little deer. Now, we are seeing more and more trophy-class deer getting killed each year – with one hotbed of trophy caliber being parts of Mississippi. They were the first to institute statewide antler point restrictions in 1995, and have evolved those regulations

HUNTER BIO | DENNIS CAMPBELL

DENNIS CAMPBELL

AGE/HOMETOWN: 62/Sumiton, Ala.

YEARS HUNTING: 50 years

FAVORITE HUNT LOCATION: On my own property in Greene County, Ala.

DEER HARVESTED: Probably 200

LARGEST BUCK: Around 140 points SCI.

FAVORITE METHOD: Stand hunting from blinds or treestands.

CONTACT INFO: www.superslam.org

WHITETAIL SLAM: Yes

TOM MIRANDA

Using double trees and multiple tree trunks allows hunters to hide more easily in treestands. Leafy camo suits have lost some popularity over the years, yet are still extremely effective concealment.

to the point where legal deer now have to meet a minimum inside spread or main beam length."

Hunters across the country are encountering varied deer management regulations at regional and statewide levels and might want to consider them when planning a trip to a certain SLAM region. They will also want to consider cover and food sources, both of which Adams commented extensively on in regards to the Southeast.

"Habitat in the Southeast consists of a lot of cover. You are also going to encounter a lot of deer food, but just because it is green that doesn't mean that it is high-quality food. In fact, much of the available deer-palatable food in the Southeast is low in nutrition. There is plenty of agriculture though, and we are blessed with a lot of forbs, which the deer love. Forbs tend to do well when they are hit with sunlight, which is often the case when timber is removed from a property. You can go from poor to no food in a certain area, to having quality forbs sprouting up in a very centralized spot in the span of a year."

Traveling hunters looking to take part in a deer feeding pattern relating to freshly-sprouted forbs can use the same trick that hunters in the far north do, which is to scour aerial photos for fresh clearcuts. It takes some time to learn exactly what one of these areas looks like, but there is a trick to it. If you know where a fresh clearcut is, or an area in the Southeast where the pines have recently been logged, simply look it up on Google Earth or other aerial photo website and take note of how it looks. Other recently cut areas will have a similar appearance in earth tones, shadows and overall look. These are the spots you should visit on a scouting trip to see if the deer are using them as anticipated.

Food is the driving force for deer movement 11 months of the year and the Southeast is no exception. The hunter that learns to identify preferred food sources all season long will simply be in a better position to intercept traveling whitetails; no matter what region he or she hunts. In deer hunting, it's the little details that make all of the difference, and knowing which plants make the local deer salivate is definitely one of them.

The Southeastern whitetail might not be your first choice for a traveling hunt, but few areas are more rewarding to outsmart a mature buck. Liberal tags, long seasons and a plethora of viable tactics await the hunter willing to test his mettle against these heavily-pressured whitetails.

SEMINOLE WHITETAIL

(Odocoileus virginianus seminolus)

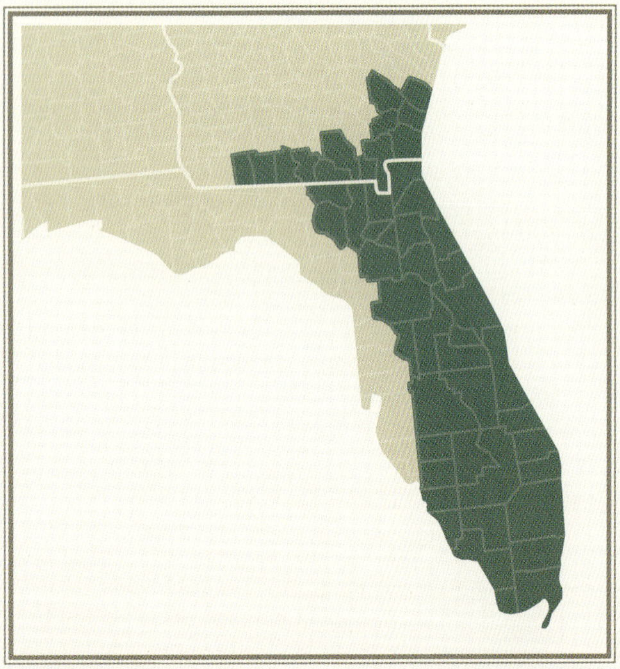

Deer in the Northern Woodlands, South-Central Plains and Dakota Regions dominate the thoughts and dreams of most die-hard whitetail hunters just as much as deer from the Seminole territory slip completely from most acknowledgement. After all, who wants to don their camouflage duds and hunt in a place known more for bikinis and beach life?

The answer depends on many things, but to overlook the Seminole whitetail because of preconceived notions of the state is a common mistake. By far, the vast majority of hunters who travel to the Seminole region have either Osceola turkeys in mind, or nearly as likely, the feral hogs that have adapted so well to swamp life. In fact, many of the invasive species like Burmese pythons, piranhas and even giant African land snails receive far more ink and attention than the small deer that inhabit the region, which is testament to the delicate balance of ecosystem, media sensationalism, and a pure lack of interest.

Fortunately for any hunter interested in completing a Whitetail SLAM, or the Ultimate SLAM, the possibility to hunt the Seminole Region is very real, and shouldn't be as intimidating as it seems on the surface. If you do decide a trip to the region is in your future, the best bet is to arm yourself with as much education as possible about the deer, what they eat, and how they conduct themselves in their chosen habitats. Sounds a bit similar to deer across the country, doesn't it?

A BASAL KNOWLEDGE

Few people in the entire country, or the world for that matter, possess as much knowledge on the Seminole whitetail as Quality Deer Management Association's Kip Adams. Adams spent a good portion of his higher education years in the heart of the Seminole territory, and has a soft spot in his heart for the deer that live there.

TONY J PETERSON

Not all deer hunting involves giant-racked bucks. Although some of the mature deer in the Seminole Region end up sporting impressive racks, hunters don't travel to the region for a Booner – they go for the challenge and the experience.

"I love the Seminole whitetails because they are so different from many of the other subgroups, especially the deer that have evolved to get as heavy as possible in the summer and fall so they can live off of their fat supplies throughout the winter. Florida deer don't need a big fat supply to live off of, and they don't have those big weight swings that other whitetails farther north experience. In fact, even captive deer lose weight in the winter, even when they have adequate food and no stress, simply because of how they have evolved. Not Seminole deer though."

If Adams' words don't point to the need for a differentiation between different subgroups of whitetails, it's hard to understand what could. To not experience the weight fluctuations and heavy feeding periods like its northern cousins means that the life cycle of the Seminole deer differs greatly from others and deserves its own designation.

Understanding all of this is a good start to slipping an arrow or bullet into a Seminole buck. "Underestimating these deer is a bad idea, because although they might not grow as big of antlers as their northern counterparts, they are every bit as wary and are extremely challenging. This is due largely to the habitat they live in."

Palmettos, sand flats, oak hammocks, long-leaf pine woods and swamps comprise much of the Seminole's favorite haunts. In other words, chokingly-thick plant life punctuated by gator-filled swamps are likely to greet the traveling hunter, which begs a question of

The Seminole Region is one of the most overlooked areas to hunt whitetail bucks. Although body size is small compared to northern deer, Seminole whitetails can grow big racks and will offer as much challenge as any deer, anywhere.

further knowledge and safety before ever setting foot in Seminole territory. Just like drawing a coveted bighorn sheep or mountain goat tag, success with any weapon starts with a clear acknowledgement of what you need to prepare for. A wary deer in a wide-open deciduous forest is no easy prey animal, but that same deer ghosting through impeding vegetation in a humid Florida swamp becomes a new challenge altogether.

Local environments are part of the experience, and so are the intricacies of different subgroups. "One unique thing about the Seminole Region is that the rut covers about eight months of the year. Basically, you can find rutting activity from July through February." As Adams points out, that amount of activity for two-thirds of the year provides an opportunity to hunt rutting deer when much of the country's whitetails aren't anywhere near breeding stages. In fact, during much of the Seminole rut, most of the rest of the country is closed to hunting, which is a great reason to add a swamp-dwelling Seminole buck to your SLAM list.

Of his personal hunting experience in the Seminole Region Adams said, "Coming from the North I never really grew accustomed to hunting in Florida. It was always so warm, which takes some getting used to." Warm or downright hot weather tends to a be a deer-movement killer throughout much of the whitetail's range, but it pays to remember that is what the Seminole deer deal with nearly every day of their lives. Hunters visiting the region should plan for hot, humid weather and dress accordingly. This also necessitates a

ISTOCK

ALL ABOUT THE SEMINOLE

BY DR. HARRY JACOBSON

RANGE

Our Seminole whitetail subgroup area has been traditionally inhabited by the subspecies O.v. seminolus (often called the Florida whitetail). The diminutive Florida Key deer occupies the islands off the southern tip of Florida, whereas the Seminole whitetail inhabits the freshwater marshes of the Everglades, southern prairie, swamps, pine-saw palmetto flatwoods, citrus orchards and some pine upland habitat in west-central and southern Florida.

RUT TIMING

Rut timing in Florida is a fascinating aspect of how deer have evolved to maximize survival. In states to the north of Florida, rut behavior of males is highly synchronized (rut timing is triggered by photoperiodism, or day length, in the South as well as the North. Think of it as the same clock but with a different time set for the alarm to go off. This changes as you get closer to the equator and there is less distinction in day length). However, in Florida and other tropical regions, breeding is not as synchronized and occurs in all months. Breeding dates for Seminole deer peak in August and September, whereas Key deer are much less synchronous in their breeding, and may drop fawns in every month of the year.

This variability indicates that the reproductive patterns of Florida's deer have evolved to unique environmental pressures. For instance, peak periods of fawning in the Everglades in southern Florida have been found to occur during the January to March dry season. Fawns from northern states are typically born during June, a period of heavy rainfall and seasonal flooding in south Florida. Females that do not become pregnant during their first estrus will come into estrus again 21 to 29 days later. As a result of this and milder climates in general, breeding in Florida may occur over much longer periods than seen among northern herds.

PHYSICAL CHARACTERISTICS

Adult Seminole whitetail bucks weigh an average of 125 pounds, generally have narrow antler spreads, and stand 36 inches high at the shoulder. Pelage is short, a dark-red-tinged shade in summer and gray to yellowish-red in winter. These deer are well adapted to climate and environment – smaller body size is beneficial in warm climates because it allows for less energy to be expended for regulating body heat.

The Key deer or Toy deer (subspecies O.v. clavium) is another Florida deer that is the smallest of all white-tailed deer, and inhabit the Keys. Bucks range from 28 to 32 inches at the shoulder and weigh an average of 80 pounds, while does stand 24 to 28 inches at the shoulder and weigh an average of 65 pounds. Key deer are listed as endangered under the U.S. Endangered Species Act, thus protected from hunting.

Hunters like Florida's Jorge Pernas prefer climbing stands when chasing Seminole whitetails, due to the fact that they can quickly set up and move locations if sightings and sign dictate a change of scenery.

TONY J PETERSON

HUNTING TIP: **LAND FOR ALL**

There is a common perception that the entire state of Florida has been bought up by retirees and wealthy beach-lovers, but that's far from the truth. Florida has millions of acres of public hunting ground, much of which offers hunters the chance to tag out on a Seminole buck. While researching potential hotspots, consider the differing regulations on the various tracts of ground throughout your chosen area. If you run into confusion or need some insight, consider contacting the Florida Fish and Wildlife Conservation Commission, which has an extensive wildlife biology division.

clear understanding of how to keep scent to a minimum when sweating is a certainty.

It's no secret that hunting the Seminole Region will mean spending stand time in hot weather, but exactly what forage to target might be more of a mystery. Adams discovered through his research in the region that just like with the Southeastern Region, while food may be everywhere, much of it is low quality. "In Florida, the soil is poor, which results in food that is nutritionally weak even though it's everywhere. This means that the deer there can fill up their bellies quickly, but the food will take a long time to digest and course through

Bloody arrows and bowhunting success aren't as uncommon as you'd think in Florida. The Seminole Region offers a deer hunting experience that varies greatly from much of the whitetail's range.

TONY J PETERSON

their system."

Few hunters in the Seminole Region understand what foods the deer prefer more than Jorge Pernas, who has spent a great deal of time hunting the region. His tactic for finding the right food involves something borrowed from other hunters across the country. "What I'm looking for in food sources are farms or orchards. It's simple, but I want to hunt deer either on a farm, or very near a farm because they will key on what's being grown there. The farms also offer an added benefit because the deer that frequent them seem to be much more tolerant of human scent. Catching a whiff of workers all day long seems to dull their caginess when it comes to human scent, and can be a great asset if you plan to hunt them in these areas."

Pernas' advice on human scent is spot-on and is similar to methods used throughout the country by devout whitetail hunters. Every year, giant whitetails are killed in suburbs, on the boundaries of public parks and other areas where the number one predator identifying sense is dulled by over-exposure, which causes bucks to drop their guard more than deer that only smell humans when they are being hunted.

"When I get onto farm ground, or land that bor-

TONY J PETERSON

Success in the Seminole Region often involves getting into places other hunters ignore.

HUNTER BIO | JORGE PERNAS

JORGE PERNAS

AGE/HOMETOWN: 38/Miami, Fla.

YEARS HUNTING: 13 years

FAVORITE HUNT LOCATION: Sebring, Fla.

DEER HARVESTED: 17 bucks and 30 does

LARGEST BUCK: 186 7/8 inches

FAVORITE METHOD: Bowhunting

WHITETAIL SLAM:
Yes and working on an Ultimate SLAM.

TONY J PETERSON

HUNTING TIP:
THE WETTER THE BETTER

Florida is famous for many things, one of which is the prevalence of water in its vast amounts of oceanic shoreline, lakes, ponds, swamps and rivers. Truly, water is everywhere. This does two things for the traveling hunter. The first is that it often forces deer movement, and the second is that it allows adventurous souls the chance to leave other hunters behind. Even knee-deep water is a deterrent to most hunters, meaning if you're willing to wear hip or chest waders you can probably leave most hunting pressure behind. Just be very careful to check the depth of any body of water you plan to wade across, and to keep an eye out for alligators and snakes.

TONY J. PETERSON

Hunters looking to leave the crowds behind in search of a Seminole buck can don waders and cross swamps and waterways – always making sure to stay safe and keep an eye out for gators and snakes.

ders a farm, I look for travel corridors to and from the food. This is because I want to ensure my best shot at daylight movement. Our deer are very easy to turn nocturnal, and that starts with the actual food sources. Finding a mature buck moving in daylight throughout agriculture might be nearly impossible, but I might catch him moving along a trail through the thick vegetation on his way to or from the food.

"Of course, if you don't have a farm to hunt you can still plant food plots. This has become more popular here, but for me – I'd rather focus on mast trees if I can get away with it. I try to find oak tees that are going to drop throughout the season and monitor them

One thing you're sure to encounter if you hunt the Seminole Region is heat. The sun is relentless, which can make dealing with scent control a major task.

TONY J PETERSON

with trail cameras to see if the deer are using them." This method probably sounds familiar to most whitetail hunters, and points to an underlying theme in all whitetail hunting – which is that although the deer in Florida are quite different from deer in northern Minnesota, they are often hunted the same way.

Throughout the whitetail's home ranges, each has individual proclivities but can still be painted with a broad brush as far as hunting tactics are concerned. Every deer is driven by basic needs, and hunters exploit those needs in similar ways throughout the entirety of its range.

One of those tactics that is popular in about half of the states is baiting, and Floridian hunters can use feeders and corn piles in the Seminole Region provided they are hunting private land. "Baiting can be effective, but a lot of times what happens is that you set your bait site and soon the pigs overrun the bait. Once a sounder of hogs claims your feeder or bait site, the deer will choose to ignore it. This can be an expensive and frustrating way to try to hunt. Some hunters choose to fence their feeders off to try to keep the pigs out while allowing the deer in. This is a lot of work but can be productive, but personally it's not my favorite.

"I prefer food plots with clover, brassicas, sunflowers or even peas. I don't like feeders filled with corn because the bucks can grow wise to hunter presence quickly, and corn helps deer produce body heat. They

ISTOCK

Often the best hunting areas in the South are where pine plantations meet natural oaks. Florida's unique habitat is so dense that most deer are taken on crop edges or pasture.

HUNTER BIO KIP ADAMS

KIP ADAMS

AGE/HOMETOWN: 43/Knoxville, Pa.

YEARS HUNTING: 31 years

FAVORITE HUNT LOCATION:
Tioga County, Pa.

DEER HARVESTED: 75

LARGEST BUCK:
130-inch-class, 260 pounds live weight.

FAVORITE METHOD: Bowhunting

CONTACT INFO:
QDMA.com
Whitetail Properties TV

WHITETAIL SLAM:
Not yet, I have three out of four.

TONY J PETERSON

Due to the nature of the Seminole whitetail and the varying habitat, hunters can find rutting deer to hunt with any weapon of their choice.

don't need any more heat here, and although they will eat it, corn doesn't seem to be the huge draw that it is in other places.

That's not to say the deer won't use it, especially does and young bucks. This does provide the chance to set up off of a feeder and try to catch a mature buck either scent checking the bait site, or staging up in the thick stuff before he visits it."

RUT HERE, RUT THERE

Pernas chooses to hunt different areas of the state according to peak rut activity. Being a Florida resident with plenty of home-state hunting experience has given him the confidence to understand when certain areas will be filled with rut-crazed bucks, while others will be dead in the rut department. This is something a resident can take for granted, but a traveling hunter should research extensively.

"If you're hunting from about the southern end of Lake Okeechobee and farther south, you want to be on stand from the end of July through at least mid-August. In the central part of the state you'll encounter a very pronounced rut from mid- to late October. As that winds down, I start thinking about traveling farther north, because the rut will kick in there around mid-November. By January, you'll want to make your way toward the panhandle, or close to the Gulf Coast Region to take advantage of the breeding season."

The various areas of the state that Pernas hunts not only offer the chance to find the rut at different times of the year, they also offer the opportunity to hunt with various weapons starting with archery tackle and muzzleloaders, and ending with a full firearms season. If you're dead-set on hunting a Seminole Region deer, consider this last bit of advice from Pernas.

"I hardly ever call and never use a decoy. Some of the Midwestern and Eastern whitetail tactics seem to spook far more deer than they draw in. Experience has caused me to be very judicious with any calls or scents, instead prompting me to truly hunt for the deer instead of setting up and drawing them in. One way I

do this is by walking in during the first few minutes of daylight, as opposed to getting into my stands in the pitch dark. This way I can hunt the whole way in and use the vegetation as my cover to still-hunt to my stand. It seems counter-productive, but I killed a great buck with a muzzleloader doing this.

"I also use climbing stands and small, personal blinds a lot. I use the climbers to get into palm trees and then use the fronds to brush-in my position, just as I do with natural ground blinds. This style of hunting allows me to observe an area or a specific trail, and then fine-tune my site depending on deer movement. This isn't quite as important on private ground, but is something I live by when I hunt public land like the Big Cypress National Preserve."

The Seminole Region probably ranks near the bottom of the list as far as desirable areas to deer hunt, but that doesn't mean it should be written off completely. No other region offers as wide of diversity as far as hunt timing and peak rut fluctuations, and if you've got an adventurous soul and a willingness to think outside-of-the-box, the Seminole whitetail might be the right fit for you.

This is especially true for Gulf Coast and Southeastern Region residents, who will only have to travel a relatively short distance to hunt the swamp-dwelling deer of the Seminole Region. Just remember to carefully consider pre-planning and mentally prepare for a hotter-than-average stand sit. Leap that mental hurdle though, and you just might find yourself enjoying your deer hunting time spent in a swaying palm tree while rutting bucks crisscross a nearby swamp in mid-August.

CHAPTER 7

GULF COAST WHITETAIL

(Odocoileus virginianus mcilhennyi and Odocoileus virginianus osceola)

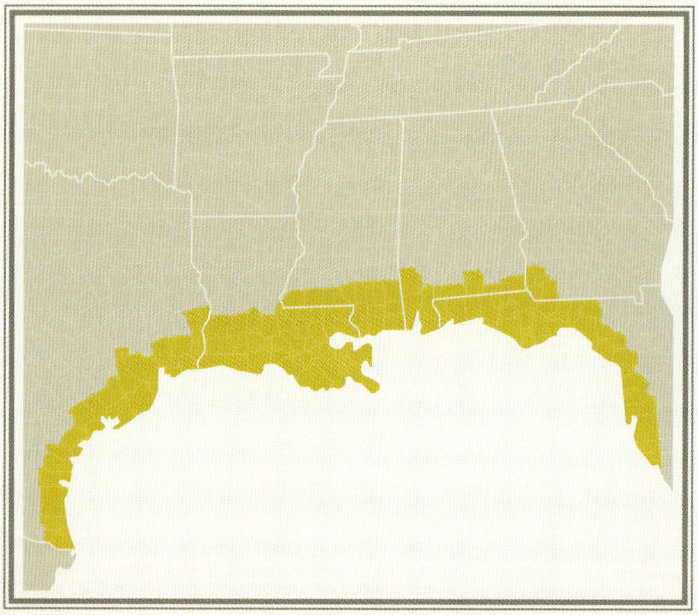

Similar to the deer found in the Seminole Region, Gulf Coast whitetails don't receive quite as much love as those found to the north. This is understandable considering most whitetail hunters simply don't equate hunting deer with warm weather, and if they do it is almost always viewed as a necessary evil.

Gulf Coast deer live up to their name, inhabiting a thin buffer zone that follows the Gulf of Mexico coastline from southern Texas to Florida. Hunters visiting this region are far more likely to be packing sunscreen and fishing rods than bows and arrows or high-caliber rifles. However, writing off these coastal deer might be a bad idea, especially if you're interested in a SLAM.

Since the range of these deer is relatively thin and covers several whitetail-friendly states, attaining a half-slam in one trip is not out of the question. This is probably most doable in Texas, but it would be a mistake to overlook opportunities in Alabama, Mississippi and even Louisiana.

If you think a Gulf Coast whitetail hunt may be in your future, consider boning up on their habitats and behaviors. Unlike a Northern Woodlands hunter traveling to Iowa for a South Central Plains deer, most hunters traveling to the Gulf Coast Region will have very limited resources and knowledge about hunting there. This isn't meant as a discouragement, just a reminder that when traveling to parts unknown, any legwork and research conducted at the front end will make things easier on the back end.

As a last caveat to the Gulf Coast whitetail, consider that in many of the areas the rut occurs very late in the year, sometimes toward the end of January. This opens up the possibility of traveling from the Midwest or East after many of the hunting seasons are completely wrapped up. After all, who doesn't want to extend their deer hunting season?

JBMVPHOTOGRAPHY.COM

In a relatively thin strip that starts in southeastern Texas and ends in western Florida, hunters will find an extreme challenge in the Gulf Coast subgroup of whitetails.

Bird-dogging behavior is a sure sign of the rut. In the Gulf Coast territory the rut is the latest of all subgroups, typically occurring in January and February.

ALL ABOUT THE GULF COAST WHITETAILS

BY DR. HARRY JACOBSON

RANGE

These deer are present from the Panhandle of Florida into Alabama, Mississippi and Louisiana, to the coastal regions of Texas.

RUT TIMING

Perhaps the most striking differences among the deer across these state coastal areas are the variations in rut timing, which ultimately result in amazing opportunity for hunters to capitalize on peak-ruts while only traveling short distances.

The osceola subspecies in the Florida Panhandle breeds in February and March with a peak of Feb. 21.

The osceola subspecies in coastal Alabama breeds from late December through February with a peak between Jan. 18 and 23.

In coastal Mississippi the mcilhennyi subspecies breeds from Jan. 16 to Feb. 6 with a peak date of Jan. 24.

The peak of mcilhennyi breeding in coastal Louisiana is Dec. 14 - 29.

Texas had two study areas in their Gulf Prairie and Marshes Ecological Region. In the northern part the peak of breeding was Sep. 30. In the southern part of the region the peak was Oct. 31.

PHYSICAL CHARACTERISTICS

In general, with the exception of more fertile Delta areas, Gulf Coast deer are smaller in body size than inland deer populations. This may be in part due to poor soil fertility along much of the Gulf Coast. Here, mature bucks range from 130 to 170 pounds live body weight. Despite smaller body size, some of these animals can still sport very impressive antlers. They have short pelage, which in the winter may take on a "grizzled" appearance. Habitat and environmental differences cause these wide variations in body size and rut timing across not only the broad Gulf region, but on a micro level in areas relatively close in proximity.

WELCOME TO THE JUNGLE

One of the first things that will strike anyone who happens to hunt the Gulf Coast territory for the first time is the thickness of vegetation. Year-round growing seasons and other favorable conditions come together to create a perfect storm of choking flora, and although it can seem a detriment to deer hunting, in reality it's a good thing. Mississippi resident Dean Scott understands this well.

"Our habitat is nasty, gnarly, and generally really thick. There are many places where you simply can't walk through the vegetation, especially in areas where the timber has been cut. When 'cutovers' are in the early stages of re-growth – vines, jasmine, honeysuckle and other plants just take over. They become sanctuaries that the deer love to use, so even if thickets of this type are impossible to enter and hunt, they still play into hunting strategy.

"Since our habitat is so thick, we don't have a lot of agriculture to hunt. I end up relying heavily on oak trees, especially those that I call 'early droppers.' Our bow season opens in mid-October, and finding an early dropper is one of my favorite scenarios for tagging out during early season. Occasionally, timber cutters will leave oak trees as seed trees, which is an ideal setup be-

Although it's far from a typical whitetail hunting destination, willing hunters can find a truly unique opportunity to chase deer in the Gulf Coast Region.

JBMVPHOTOGRAPHY.COM

SETTING GOALS

Bowhunting success in the whitetail woods year in and year out requires planning and a specific skill set. Often, bowhunters strive to pattern and kill a mature buck on their home hunting ground, and spend countless hours running trail cameras and building food plots. Other hunters strive to take only large-racked bucks, and their goal is to find and harvest a Booner every fall.

More and more hunters are finding that the challenges of traveling to hunt whitetails are fun and offer a chance to see new territory and hunt different deer. For a hunter in New England to travel to Montana and hunt a western whitetail is an entirely new experience. High-plains bucks are a different deer than their northern woodland cousins. For an Ohio hunter, rattling bucks into bow range in Kansas or Texas can be a chance to experience the thrill of luring a shooter buck across a half mile of CRP field or pear flat to find the mock fight.

Whatever your hunting goals are, you'll need a full-season strategy to be successful. The best hunters use a methodical approach to locating and patterning bucks. The most successful deer hunters aren't always the best hunters – they are the most prepared hunters. An effective whitetail strategy is a 12-month process.

That is something every traveling hunter needs to take into account. For example, the northern Missouri resident used to seeing big-bodied, heavy-racked bucks that decides to try his hand at the Gulf Coast Region is going to be in for a bit of a culture shock. Gone will be his agricultural fields and deciduous forests, which will be replaced by wall-thick vegetation and miles of contiguous cover. Gone too, will be the real possibility of encountering a giant buck, as far as inches of antler are concerned.

Some regions do not produce huge racks, and even if they did, very few people would kill the bucks sporting them. That's the nature of our sport and even though we commonly see 200-inch bucks in hook-and-bullet magazines and on outdoor television, they are still extremely rare. Know long before you ever travel to a new spot what kind of deer would make you happy.

For many hunters on limited budgets and with time constraints, any buck might suffice. As long as it makes you happy, then that is all that matters. Too often we get hung up on huge racks to the detriment of our hunting enjoyment, and the minute measurement-obsession starts to erode the fun, discontent sets in and it's very hard to get the pleasure back.

WINDIGO IMAGES

HUNTING TIP:
BECOME ONE WITH NATURE

Although it sounds like a hippie philosophy, hunters can take a lesson from the granola-crunching crowd and try to better transition into the wooded environments. Florida's David Brooks abides by this philosophy when he pursues the Gulf Coast whitetails near his home. "You know you've got it right when birds are landing near you and the squirrels aren't barking. You've successfully become part of the environment and that's important."

You can take cues from the animals around you and recognize whether you're hidden well enough and that you're movements are at a tolerable level. Deer pay attention to the alarm calls and behaviors of all of the animals around them, and something as simple as a ticked-off squirrel may cause an approaching buck enough anxiety to turn around, or at the very least spend much more time figuring out what set the rodent off in the first place.

cause only a few trees will be left in a cutover. I recently found this situation and took a mature eight-pointer that was keying on one of the two oaks that were left."

Scott brings up an interesting point that is often overlooked by hunters in the Midwest and East where oak trees are extremely common. Simply finding an oak ridge or a patch of oak trees does not ensure deer hunting success. Finding the exact tree deer prefer is much more important and boils down to a few things. The first is recognizing the differences between tree varieties. We all know that deer prefer white oak acorns over red oak acorns, but that is far from all you need to know.

There are dozens of oak tree species in the United States, and they vary greatly from region to region. Knowing what trees produce the most favorable acorns and at what times will make you a better hunter any time you're near these deciduous deer magnets. It's also important to note that while deer prefer a certain acorn, they may eventually devour all of the acorns in a certain area. Hunters in the northern part of the United States are likely to witness this as their deer vacuum white acorns immediately, and then as agricultural food sources disappear and winter sets in, they'll start

DENNIS CAMPBELL

Grand Slam Club director Dennis Campbell shows off a south Alabama Gulf Coast buck from 1986.

HUNTER BIO DEAN SCOTT

DEAN SCOTT

Dean Scott pictured with son Lucas.

AGE/HOMETOWN: 47/Lucedale, Miss.

YEARS HUNTING: 41 years

FAVORITE HUNT LOCATION:
South Mississippi swamps and South Kansas.

DEER HARVESTED:
Over 50 in multiple states.

LARGEST BUCK:
192 inches, 309 pounds live weight.

FAVORITE METHOD:
Bowhunting from treestands.

CONTACT INFO: www.the3rdarm.com

WHITETAIL SLAM: No

Spanish moss hanging from gnarly oaks is Gulf Coast habitat, while a good buck surveys his surroundings.

Jamie Satterfield bowhunts the early season. Notice the ThermaCELL® unit on his hip. ThermaCELL® insect protection is a must in Southeastern, Gulf Coast and Seminole territories, and will not spook deer as it effectively deters mosquitoes.

feeding on red oak ridges to take advantage of the less-desirable acorns.

Scott keyed on his oak tree knowledge to arrow that big Mississippi buck, but the catalyst for his hunt started with a single set of big tracks on a gravel road that leads to his hunting camp. "One day when I was driving in I saw big tracks going into an isolated block of timber by the highway and near some houses. I could actually hear kids playing the night I shot him, and realized that he had holed up in a place that none of the other hunters paid any attention to."

GULF COAST HUNT TIMING

According to Scott the middle of the season is not the best time to plan a hunt. "Our midseason is very dead. It's just like the lull farther north, but ours occurs in November and December. We still hunt our food plots on the off chance of catching a hungry buck making a mistake, but for the most part it's pretty slow. To up my odds of running into a mature buck, I spend a lot of my time hunting staging areas off of our food plots. Our deer get hunted pretty hard and that's part of the reason we have such a dead stretch. Occasionally, I'll find a buck that will stage-up 70 or 80 yards from the food plots and that's where I'll get my shot. It's far from

Gulf Coast hunter David Brooks has taken several good-sized bucks on public land, which is no small feat. His secret to success is multi-faceted, but relies heavily on scouting harder than the competition.

a sure-thing, but better than not hunting."

As December comes to a close and the new year creeps ever closer, hunters in the Gulf Coast Region will start to see increasing rut activity. Rubs and scrapes will show up on trails and the edges of food plots, and the odds of connecting on a bruiser increase steadily throughout the month of January. A hunt planned any time during the first month of the year should ensure a better chance at tagging out on a buck.

LEAVE THE CALLS, BRING THE WADERS

Local experience trumps most research and preconceived notions, and Scott has some advice for those willing to travel to the Gulf Coast. "These deer are cagier than Midwest deer in my experience. Because of that I don't call or decoy much. I still carry a grunt tube with me in case I see a buck that doesn't seem like he plans on heading in my direction, but generally I keep many of the tactics common in the Midwest to an absolute minimum. This is not to say that you can't rattle, grunt or snort-wheeze, but for me the best success comes from figuring out where the bucks want to travel and getting in there with a good wind."

Just how Scott "gets in there" might surprise some, but the reality is that Gulf Coast hunters are going to spend their time at extremely low elevations, which means that water is always a factor. "We deal with flooding a lot. In fact, this past year our river bottom flooded and it basically sealed off one of our food plots. I kept thinking about that plot out there, not getting any pressure, and I decided to put on my son's duck hunting waders and hunt it. The plot was basically an island of grass surrounded by water of varying depths. And it was covered in deer sign.

"I sat there that afternoon and could hear deer splashing all over. Eventually I saw three different shooters that got dangerously close, but stayed just out of range. Even though I didn't kill one, it was a learning experience and absolutely cool evening on stand."

It's a safe bet that Scott will eye up his hunting ground year in and year out to find similar situations

Young Lucas Scott of Mississippi's low country knows how to hunt Gulf Coast bucks.

that require thinking outside-of-the-box and a little extra sweat equity. This is just another example of the mindset necessary to continually outsmart mature bucks – regardless of region. From the nearly treeless regions at the far northern boundary of the whitetail's range, to a coast known more for tailing redfish than deer, hunters willing to try new things and satisfy curiosities are rewarded just enough to keep doing what others won't.

PUBLIC GULF BUCKS

Certain areas of the Dakota, Northern Woodlands and Northwestern Regions all have huge tracts of public land that are perfect for the do-it-yourself whitetail hunter. It would be easy to look at the map of the Gulf Coast Region and assume that there probably aren't quality areas of public land big enough to accommodate many hunters, but in some cases that assumption would be wrong.

David Brooks, who hails from northwestern Florida, is a devout public land hunter who has taken plenty of bucks with his archery equipment. When asked of the

HUNTER BIO | DAVID BROOKS

AGE/HOMETOWN: Niceville, Fla.

YEARS HUNTING: 35 years

FAVORITE HUNT LOCATION:
Okaloosa County, Fla.
and Butler County, Ky.

DEER HARVESTED: 80

LARGEST BUCK:
124 3/8 inches, 130 pounds Florida. And 121 inches, 235 pounds from Illinois.

FAVORITE METHOD: Archery

WHITETAIL SLAM: Yes

Public land hunter, David Brooks, has honed his scouting and hunting down to the point where he continually tags out on good bucks in the Gulf Coast Region.

key to his success, Brooks had plenty to say. "I scout a lot, but no matter where I'm going to hunt down here I take a long look at the area on Google Earth. One of the areas I hunt consists of 350,000 acres and a lot of the timber on the property was cut at the turn of the century and then re-planted with fast-growing pines. Those pines are old-growth now. The place has no agriculture and is table-top flat so I take all of those factors into account and scour aerial photos for transition areas."

Just like the northern Michigan hunter looking for the right age class of clearcut, Brooks spends his time trying to identify strips of timber with clearcuts in the four- or five-year-old class. Where these areas meet creates an edge, or transition, and whitetails are notorious for using these areas to their advantage not only to feed, but also to travel. Brooks highlights a few of these spots on his maps and then laces up his hunting boots for on-the-ground scouting.

"I like to burn boot leather whenever I can. Once I've identified a few likely looking areas, I get out there and look around for sign. If the sign is convincing enough, I'll hang a few cameras to monitor the area when I back out. I then try to minimize my intrusion to keep the deer at ease. If my cameras show some promise, I'll typically stay out of the area until much closer to the season and then I'll walk it again, although this time I'm looking for hunter activity. I want to see if anyone else has hung stands in there or if there are any boot tracks in the mud. My goal is to find a transition area that other hunters have overlooked."

The method of out-hunting the competition is common amongst public land hunters, but is sometimes lost on private ground hunters. Certain places, especially those where you've gained access through permission, might feature as much pressure as public land in other areas. The perception is that private is always better than public, but if every field-edge corner has a stand and a steady stream of weekend warriors on it, the private designation doesn't mean squat if you don't figure out how to beat the competition.

Brooks takes this to another level in his scouting by spending as much time as possible sleuthing around during June and July. Both months are ridiculously hot and humid, which keeps the competition suppressed. His willingness to work up a sweat and get out there when others stay home to enjoy their air conditioning is what sets him apart from many of the other hunters in his area.

"My whole goal is just to find a spot that has one

Top bowhunters mark broadhead tipped arrows that fly true in practice for confidence and accuracy on the hunt, especially in areas like the Gulf Coast Region where earning a single shot at a mature buck might take all season.

TOM MIRANDA

or two mature bucks and no people. I'm competitive as hell, but over the years I've buddied-up with a few guys who hunt just like I do. We now share trail camera photos and scouting information to make the process easier."

It's no secret that the Gulf Coast draws hoards of spring breakers and beach-oriented vacationers, but living close to the ocean's edge is a subgroup of whitetails few hunters would even consider hunting. The right planning and research can go a long way toward securing a chance at one of the crafty bucks that call the region home, just be prepared for some heat, bugs and vegetation so thick you might need a machete to get through it. If that seems like a deterrent, consider that it might be enough to keep most of the weekend warriors out of the woods, but not a truly serious whitetail hunter.

HUNTING TIP: USE A GPS UNIT

Hunters traveling west to try their hand at elk or mule deer almost always carry a GPS unit. It makes sense considering the vastness of the west and the intimidation factor of the high country. Whitetail hunters don't rely on these handy units nearly as much, but they should. Considering the type of cover and the vast, flat areas of the Gulf Coast Region, it can be easy to lose landmarks and become turned around. Or, once identified, a hotspot can disappear on a return trip because there are very few terrain features to mark. The same goes for the alder thickets of the Northern Woodlands and the swamps of the Southeastern Region. Like a personal protection firearm, it's better to have a GPS and not need it, than need it and not have it. Waypoint your truck, your stand sites and fresh sign just in case.

CHAPTER 8

DAKOTA WHITETAIL

(Odocoileus virginianus dacotensis)

Using shallow rivers to enter and exit stand sites is commonplace in the Dakota Region, where many of the deer spend their time bedded in river bottoms.

TONY J PETERSON

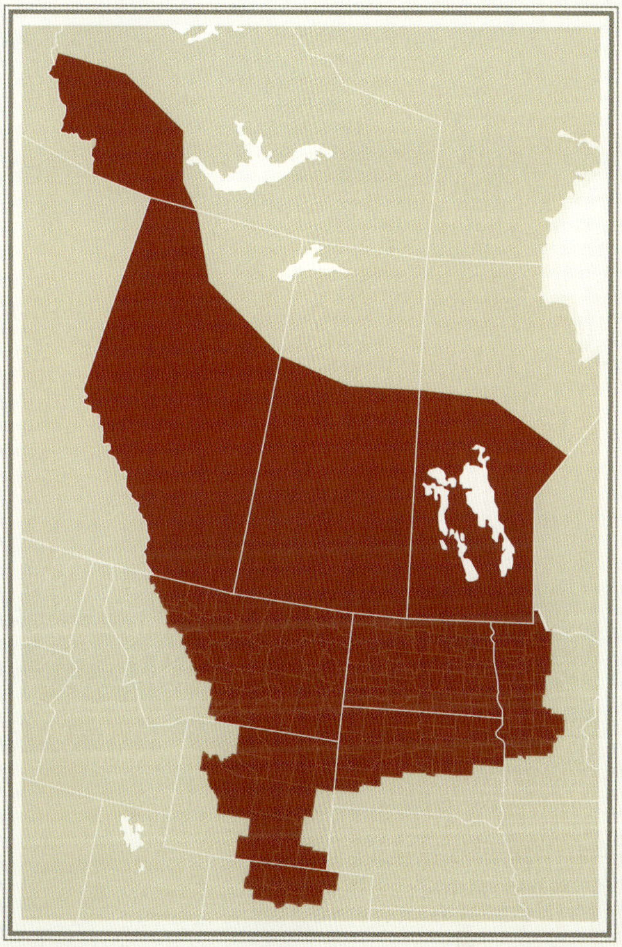

The South-Central Plains and the Northern Woodlands whitetails get a lot of the love, but it's wise not to ignore the territory that contains the Dakota whitetail. For years Montana, Wyoming and the river bottoms of North and South Dakota hosted savvy hunters to deer sightings of record proportions.

Television and print media "let the cat out of the bag" so to speak, and the hidden gem that is the Dakota whitetail suddenly hit the collective radar of deer hunters from all over. Outfitters were quick to capitalize on the opportunity and since much of the land in the Dakota region is not suitable for whitetails, the quality areas were soon sewed up.

In a matter of a few years the Dakota Region, and more specifically certain parts of Canada and the Milk and Powder Rivers in Montana, became go-to places for whitetail hunters looking for a hunt that would guarantee deer sightings and high odds of getting a shot at a mature buck.

Unlike the deer rush in big-buck states like Kansas and Iowa, though, much of the Dakota Region also

Fence crossings can be used as ambush sites as bucks can be habitual users of specific field access points.

ALL ABOUT THE DAKOTA WHITETAIL

BY DR. HARRY JACOBSON

RANGE

The Dakota whitetail is widely distributed throughout western and central Canada, Montana, Wyoming, Colorado, North and South Dakota, and western Minnesota. From Saskatchewan to the cottonwood bottoms of Montana and everywhere else in its range, the Dakota is highly prized as a game animal for its magnificent antlers, even in those western states where elk and mule deer are commonly thought of as the primary quarry.

The Dakota's range often overlaps with those of the Northwestern to the west, and of the Northern Woodland to the east – with which it shares the same capabilities of achieving great body size and antler growth.

RUT TIMING

Mid-November, when deer are in rut in the Dakota territory is an exciting time like all others, but it's unique in that bucks can be seen chasing does in the wide open prairies. In river bottoms where population concentrations are high, the action can be fast and dramatically close as the bucks get on their feet. Any time from Oct. 31 through Thanksgiving can be highly productive.

PHYSICAL CHARACTERISTICS

Although there are very few distinguishable physical differences between the Dakota whitetail and its Northwestern and Northern Woodland neighbors, the dramatic differences in hunting Dakotas in the plains, river bottoms and hills they make home is what makes traveling to hunt these deer such a worthwhile adventure. In places like Alberta and Saskatchewan, finding a mature buck in excess of 300 pounds is not at all uncommon, and some grow to be substantially larger. Throughout their habitat, the Dakota is generally one of the most impressive deer subspecies in terms of body and antler size.

offers nonresidents a chance at western species like antelope, elk and mule deer. This availability of varying species tempered the overall demand for whitetail tags and to this day there exists an awesome opportunity to hunt.

It's not just outfitters that have access to quality land either. Unlike much of the Midwest and several whitetail-packed areas of the East, the Dakota whitetails are available on public land in huge patches of state and federal properties. While it may not hold as many truly giant bucks as the Midwest, the Dakota Region offers the traveling hunter a good chance at a deer in the 120- to 150-inch range – which is nothing to scoff at.

One particular hunter who has recognized the value of this region is whitetail guru and television host, Greg Miller. "Even though I grew up hunting big-woods bucks in my home state of Wisconsin, I've fallen in love with the Dakota subspecies. The hunting experience is so different from other regions in that you actually get to watch the deer and try to get a really good pattern on them. If you spend enough time on the glass you can usually find a specific deer to target, and unlike so much of the whitetail territory, you don't have to be a student of sign interpretation."

The Dakotas and eastern Montana include a lot of wide-open habitat, and trophy buck hunters often opt for a rifle and long distance shooting. Here Mark Kayser scans the Breaks for a good buck.

The ability to watch deer with your own two eyes cannot be understated. Witnessing firsthand how deer interact with one another, and how they travel through the landscape is first-rate knowledge that will always make you a better hunter. This is part of the reason why hunters that scout a great deal almost always kill more bucks than hunters who don't spend much time in the woods. It's a common misconception that when you're scouting you're always looking for sign, or simply glassing bachelor groups in the summer. While it's true that both of those activities count as scouting, it's also important to realize that the more time you spend scouting, the more time you'll watch deer all year long.

This is no different than the hunter who only sits during the weekends as opposed to the hunter who has the opportunity to hunt for a few weeks straight. The hunter that spends unbroken time in the woods will almost always be more comfortable knowing when to move when a deer approaches and just when to take the shot. That's not to say that weekend warriors can't get it right, because they can. However, any time you spend observing deer will make you better at killing deer.

RIVER BOTTOM TRICKS

Although there is a lot of public ground in the Dakota Region that contains deer, first-time hunters often need to rethink their "needs" when it comes to killing a whitetail. Considering much of the region is home to large cattle ranches, much of the best land is also privately owned and farmed in hay or alfalfa. A lot of

TIM HERALD

Kentucky hunter Tim Herald registered this Saskatchewan giant in the pursuit of his Whitetail SLAM.

HUNTER BIO GREG MILLER

GREG MILLER

AGE/HOMETOWN: 61/Bloomer, Wis.

YEARS HUNTING: 49 years

FAVORITE HUNT LOCATION:
North and South Dakotas

DEER HARVESTED:
50 Pope and Young, over 100 total.

LARGEST BUCK:
202⅝ inches, 297 pounds live weight.

FAVORITE METHOD:
Treestand bowhunting.

CONTACT INFO:
www.millertv.net

WHITETAIL SLAM: Yes

HUNTING TIP: UP-TO-THE-MINUTE RESEARCH

In the past few years just about every whitetail hunter has heard about EHD, or Epizootic Hemorrhagic Disease, which is a nasty infectious disease caused by biting flies that can wreak havoc on localized whitetail populations. Due to drought conditions in the Dakota Region and the high concentrations of deer, certain areas are highly prone to EHD outbreaks. Although it's difficult to measure, some areas that are hit hardest by the disease seem to experience die-offs of up to 90 percent of the local herd. You can imagine how quickly that would shut down the hunting in a specific area. Although any state with whitetails can experience outbreaks, it's advisable to do some research before traveling to the Dakota Region to find out if the disease has hit your potential hunting area. A call to the nearest big-game biologist will clear things up quickly and will definitely be worth the effort. Because the disease can be so localized, a badly affected area might only consist of a relatively small section of river bottom, necessitating a change of plans from one spot to an area only 10 or 20 miles away. Either way, knowing before you ever hit the road will offer peace-of-mind.

the secondary land is grazed with cattle (both private and public). Because of this, it can be disheartening to sneak down a gravel road along a river and literally see hundreds of deer that are on private agricultural fields, while much of the public land seems to be devoid of quality food sources – and consequently devoid of deer.

There are two things you can do to remedy this problem. The first is to simply ask permission, which is something Savage Outdoors host Mike Stroff does not shy away from when he travels to South Dakota each fall. "In that river-bottom country the first thing you need to do is find the landowners who own the fields. A lot of it might be leased up, but it's still possible to find landowners willing to let you hunt. They are growing that alfalfa for their cattle and the deer eat a good chunk of it each summer and fall."

If you strike out when knocking on doors but still want to hunt deer using the agricultural fields, consult your maps. Current topographical maps will show where the private and public land meet. A lot of times

Gouged rubs are often the rule for Dakota bucks. Giant bucks in small thickets often destroy saplings.

Deer hunting is what draws traveling hunters to the Dakota Region, but the scenery is worth it as well. Shown here is an early morning image of the Little Missouri River in western North Dakota.

TONY J PETERSON

Master buck hunter Ron Cormier poses with a few of his many Pope and Young whitetail trophies.

Ohio bowhunter Adam Hays collects shed antlers during the early season to locate surviving bucks and plan strategies for upcoming hunts.

Television host Mike Stroff loves hunting South Dakota. One of his go-to methods is to build a natural blind using round bales in an alfalfa or hay field. This is a great tactic for earning a close bow shot.

there might not be much in the way of food on the public, but it might contain better bedding cover than the adjoining private land. This is especially true if the landowner grazes cattle, which is very common.

If you see this potential scenario playing out, revisit Miller's advice and load your daypack with a spotting scope, tripod and binoculars. If the deer are feeding in the fields and bedding on public ground, they will travel in a very predictable route to the fields in the evening and from the fields in the morning. A day or two of watching this should tip you into how many deer are following the pattern and where exactly they are traveling.

Even better is the situation where the deer have to cross a river to get to and from the food. This narrows down the travel routes considerably and will probably clue you into exact trees to hang stands in. That's where patterning a specific buck can get much easier because he may choose to bed in an area that's 10 acres or more, and then mill through the river bottom before crossing – but he will often use the same crossing from night to night.

Ideally, he'll cross close to a stand-friendly tree, but often the western river bottoms contain huge, old cottonwoods that frame the river and are far too large-of-trunk to accommodate a stand. In that case, it might be necessary to build a natural ground blind next to one of those giant trees, or pop up a hub-style blind and brush it in extremely well.

Another blind option, should you gain access to a private field, is something that has caught on slightly in the whitetail world and will likely keep gaining speed as more hunters recognize its effectiveness. It involves using real round hay bales and positioning them just right, a trick that Stroff uses often in South Dakota. "If the landowner will allow it, I love moving alfalfa bales in the middle of a field and position them so there is a hiding spot in the middle. For some reason, the deer seem to like to walk out to the bales. It provides the perfect chance to shoot them, and is really effective when bowhunting. We use this trick a lot when there aren't very many available stand trees."

Stroff's hay bale blind tactic is a good one, but leads to a problem. "If you're in a good field, you're going to have a lot of deer around you. This is great until it's time to leave. Just like in the rest of the country, if you blow a

Shooting sticks can help steady crosshairs on long-distance shots in the open terrain found in the Dakota Region.

DON'T FORGET THE LATE SEASON

Late season is the prime time to kill a good deer in the Dakota Region, even though most hunters look to this subspecies for an early-season hunt and the chance to tag a buck still in a very predictable pattern – and sometimes in full velvet. There are several reasons why considering a late-season foray to the region is not a bad idea. First off, hunting pressure is usually minimal to nonexistent as most bowhunters have tagged out, or won't fight the bitter temperatures and snow that often accompany a late-season hunt. Plus, nearly all of the firearms seasons are finished.

The hunters with tags left often look at the cold and snow and stay home. Those conditions that keep hunters inside, are the very same ones that drive mature bucks from their beds before dusk to seek nutrition in an effort to keep warm. Late season however, means herds of deer bunched together, and this is where the hunt becomes tricky with archery tackle. This fact is compounded even more in some areas of the region because the deer are relatively bunched up throughout the year. In the winter there can be hundreds of them in a single field, which proves exciting and challenging.

Often the deer of the late season are very spooky. They've been chased by hunters for several months and have run themselves ragged during the rut, which leaves them vulnerable to winter's unforgiving cold and snowfall. Those spooky deer are acutely aware of their surroundings, and even the slightest noise will catch their attention as cold air magnifies every minute sound; the crunch of snow or squeak of a stand will echo loudly in the woods.

During most late-season hunts, stand trees are void of canopy cover which makes utilizing an aerial set difficult. Ground blinds and covered tower stands are great choices because of their full concealment. Plus, you can employ a small portable heater, which allows for longer sits with the walls and roof protecting you from sleet, snow and bitter wind.

Often the areas where shed antlers are found in spring are good places to hunt in the late season. Look for deer yards during midwinter and plan your stands ahead of time. Farmers who winter lots of deer likely will allow hunting during late season as crop damage is a big concern in some areas. Those same farmers are more likely to give the late-season hunter permission simply because they are done hunting, as are their family and friends.

Although you might not have much in the way of competition for a late-season Dakota buck, you will have to be on your A-game, and will most likely earn your deer through the sheer tenacity it takes to sit in freezing temperatures and wait out an approaching buck.

bunch of deer out of a field you'll start to see an erosion in the amount that show up each night. That starts with mature deer and can truly kill a good spot. We work hard to find entrance and exit routes that don't expose us to all of the deer. In the instance of the hay bale blinds, we almost always have someone pick us up to blow the field out with a truck or an ATV.

"This is important even if you're only hunting for a few days. Sometimes hunters will look at a situation like that and think they can be a little sloppy considering they've only got a small amount of time to tag out. We're usually filming TV shows and literally can't afford to screw things up, so we are very careful about how we travel to and from our spots. This requires more work and more planning, but it pays off. We kill a lot of our good bucks days into a hunt because of this, and even if you're not filming, it's worth it if you really want to have a chance at a good deer."

Successful hunters throughout the entire whitetail range understand the intricacies of entrance and exit routes, but river bottoms often offer an easy way out. Plenty of western rivers that hold good whitetails are fairly shallow and can be waded easily. This allows the willing hunter the chance to don knee-high boots or hip waders and sneak through the river to and from stand sites. Often these rivers feature banks that are above the hunter's head, concealing him completely from any visual exposure. The sound of the river babbling through the landscape covers any noise, and being so low puts you in a good position wind wise. It's win, win, win for the most part but it's also important to remember to be very careful when wading any river. Make sure that it's as shallow as you hope and

HUNTING TIP:
FAMILY FIRST, DEER SECOND

It's hard to see at certain times of the fall, but serious whitetail hunters typically end up with a very supportive spouse and understanding family – or they end up alone, which is very similar to the world of professional fishing. If you've got your heart set on a Whitetail SLAM and aim to implement a traveling plan to make it happen, consider Greg Miller's advice. "If you're going to go on the road for whitetails, you better have a well-grounded relationship with your spouse and your family. In order to kill big deer consistently, you have to have support on the home front. I see it every year where hunters get so obsessed with deer that they overlook what is really important." Miller's words are spot-on and despite how amazing the experience of hunting whitetails is, it's even better when you've got a trusting, even-keel relationship with your loved ones.

HUNTER BIO JIM SHOCKEY

JIM SHOCKEY

AGE/HOMETOWN:
55/Vancouver Island, British Columbia

YEARS HUNTING: 41 years

FAVORITE HUNT LOCATION: Saskatchewan, Canada

DEER HARVESTED: Over 100

LARGEST BUCK:
Largest score, 191 inches Boone and Crockett.
Largest weight, 340 pounds.

FAVORITE METHOD:
Rattling and still-hunting.

CONTACT INFO: www.jimshockey.com

WHITETAIL SLAM: Yes

Alberta outfitter and avid bowhunter Chad Lenz with a great Alberta buck. Alberta offers great whitetail hunting opportunities for the Dakota subgroup.

that you've got a good plan for getting out in the dark, because wading an unfamiliar river under the cloak of night can make things a bit more treacherous.

LOOKING FOR A BUCK, EH?

If you take a look at the Whitetail SLAM map you'll see that the Dakota Region extends extremely far north into the Canadian provinces of Alberta, Saskatchewan and Manitoba. Each fall optimistic hunters cross the border into the land of hockey and strong beer for the chance to tag out on the biggest-bodied whitetails you're going to find anywhere.

Overall hunting uber-stud Jim Shockey has more experience hunting Canada than most, and he is particularly fond of an old-school method of taking whitetails in his home province of Saskatchewan. "In my home area you need to be flexible. You never know whether it's going to involve rattling, baiting, or even spot-and-stalk in certain situations. All of them can work, but my personal favorite involves still-hunting.

"There is nothing I love more than finding a track of a big, mature buck in fresh, powdery snow. It's not good if the snow is crusted because you'll never catch up to him, but if there is half-of-a-foot of fresh powder it's perfect. I like to find a track in the morning and set out after him. What I love about it is that they literally can't get away if you're willing to keep following them. Usually, I'll follow a buck until I feel I'm getting close and then I'll slow down to the point where I only take a step every minute or so. While I'm in this zone I also grunt, rattle and rake the brush to see if he'll show himself. It's one of the most exciting ways to hunt, and there's nothing better than knowing when you start on a track in the morning that you'll most likely run into that buck at some point throughout the day."

Shockey's tactic of getting on a track is available to hunters in the Northern Woodlands region as well, although it is something that is slipping from the modern hunter's repertoire. Years ago, getting on a track

Mathew's own Joel Maxfield is an avid buck hunter and loves to spot and stalk whitetail bucks. In his home state of Wisconsin, Joel puts bucks to bed with a spotting scope, then plans a midday stalk. His strategy is highly successful. Here Joel poses with a Montana buck.

while toting an open-sighted rifle like the Winchester Model 94 was the sign of a good hunter. Today's hunters rely much more on ambush tactics for whitetails, although there are still a few hunters who engage in the old practice.

Before you get too excited about traveling to Saskatchewan and finding a fresh set of tracks etched into the snow, it's necessary to say that you're not likely to find an outfitter that will oblige your new ambition. Shockey adds, "We guide hunters every year, but they sit on bait sites. It's too much of a liability for a nonresident to set out in the vast wildernesses we have up here. That's okay though, because when we bait we do it right and we have a high rate of success for getting visiting hunters on good deer."

The type of hunting offered in much of Canada has almost reached mythical status – due to the all-day sits in ground blinds that feature only one shooting port and the boredom that goes with it. Even hunters accustomed to cold conditions have a hard time sitting all day on Canadian hunts, and it can be absolutely brutal for hunters traveling from south of the Mason-Dixon line. However, hunters do it because the odds of killing a huge deer are high, and it only takes a single doe visiting your bait site to draw in a true monster. As in all hunting, this style can go from mind-crushing boredom and discomfort, to absolute bliss by the simple appearance of a single animal that happens to follow the script.

PRESSURE-LESS, SORT OF

Dealing with hunting pressure is just something that most hunters endure each fall. It's a part of life for most of us, and absolutely unavoidable for the public land hunter and just about any whitetail junkie living near a decent-sized city. Those hunters will fare very well in the Dakota Region, because generally speaking it prob-

ably receives less pressure than any other region, or at least exists in the top two or three for lightly-hunted deer.

This doesn't mean that the deer are pushovers, but it does mean that you might hang stands or start hunting and not have to worry about someone else blundering into your setup. This is expected on outfitted and some private land hunts, but is also possible on public ground throughout the territory. That alone is a pretty good reason to try to notch a Dakota buck on your SLAM list.

While many people envision rivers snaking their way through yellow-leafed cottonwoods and lush, green alfalfa fields, the Dakota Region offers even more splendid views than that. Broken coulees, sage flats, rolling hills and distant mountains are all highly likely on your trip to this region. Even if the deer hunting wasn't very good, visiting this part of North America would be well worth it. Of course, when you consider how good the deer hunting actually is, hunting the Dakota whitetail is an absolute no-brainer.

LEFT: Learning to shoot from a seated position limits movement and allows hunters to set stands in the shorter growth often found in the Dakota subgroup range. ABOVE: Michigan hunter Jim Benton has his Whitetail SLAM. Benton loves hunting Canadian bucks and often goes on what he calls a "Canadian Blitz" – taking whopper bucks in Manitoba, Saskatchewan and Alberta all in the same season.

CHAPTER 9

SOUTH-CENTRAL PLAINS

(Odocoileus virginianus macrourus and Odocoileus virginianus texanus)

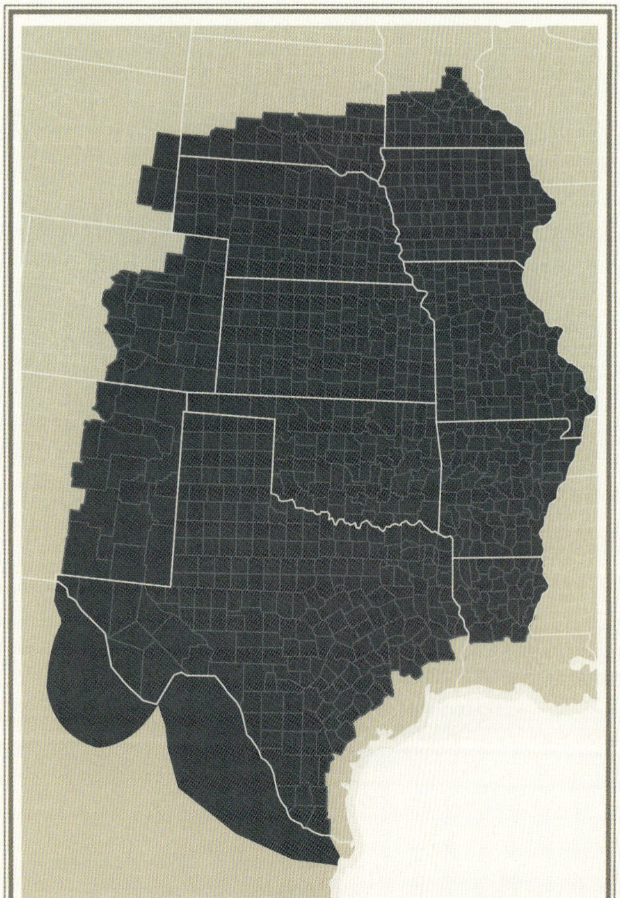

It's the holy land of whitetail hunting – the South-Central Plains Region. Stretching from the southern half of Minnesota down to Mexico, this territory undoubtedly accounts for more Booners than any other region. It's in the heart of the Midwest and contains heavy-hitting states like Iowa, Kansas and Texas.

Although the deer in the northern half of the South-Central Plains Region are considerably larger in body size than deer in the southern half, both share one thing in common that draws hunters from the entire United States – impressive antlers and in most places, a very reasonable amount of hunting pressure.

The deer hunting in certain parts of this territory has reached nearly mythical proportions, but traveling hunters would be wise to not expect a buck behind every bush. Or deer that will blindly run into every rattling sequence. The South-Central Plains whitetail is a still a whitetail, and while hunters-per-square-mile in many places will be much lower than many of the East Coast states, the deer still get hunted hard. Long seasons and an influx of nonresidents can temper some of the luster that is part of the region, but that is in no way meant to say it's not as good as anywhere in the country. In fact – without a doubt – it offers the best chance at a mature buck.

One hunter who has taken more than his fair share of those big bucks is Don Kisky. Don, along with his

TONY J PETERSON

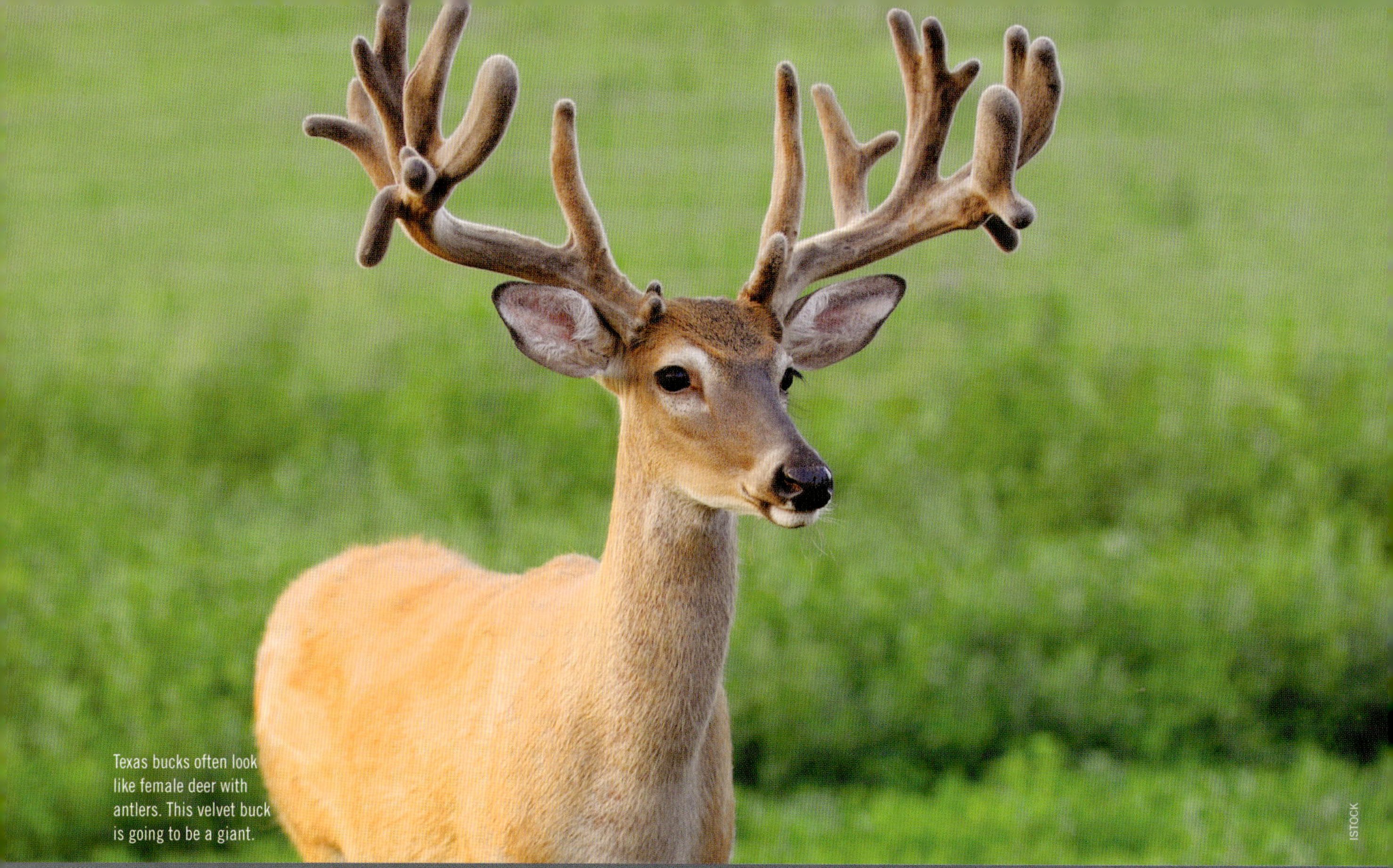

Texas bucks often look like female deer with antlers. This velvet buck is going to be a giant.

ISTOCK

ALL ABOUT THE SOUTH-CENTRAL PLAINS DEER

BY DR. HARRY JACOBSON

RANGE

Whitetail SLAM recognizes two subspecies of whitetails in its South-Central Plains category. O.v. macrourus inhabits Nebraska, Kansas, Oklahoma, Arkansas, the Texas panhandle, Missouri, and parts of Iowa, Colorado and New Mexico.

O.v. texanus, "the Texas whitetail," dwells in the gulf prairies, oak savannas, and mesquite and brush country of the South Texas Plains to the mountains of the Big Bend. Texas, unlike many states, has always valued whitetails heavily as a resource and tourist attraction. Sound herd and buck management practices have created hunting lands with some of the highest potential for both numbers of deer, and trophy harvest. The Edwards Plateau in the center of the state has high deer densities with as many as 40 per square mile.

RUT TIMING

With the exception of Texas, peak breeding for the South-Central Plains whitetail is fairly uniform across this vast area ranging from Nov. 6 to 25. Nebraska: Nov. 10-15, Kansas: Nov. 15-17, Oklahoma: Nov. 14-19, Missouri: Nov. 6-22, Iowa: Nov. 13-18, Arkansas: Nov. 18-25.

The Texas Parks and Wildlife Department has published peak breeding dates online for the eight ecological zones in the state. Breeding peaks ranged from as early as Nov. 7 to as late as Dec. 24. The latest breeding peak was in South Texas. If you're planning a deer hunting trip to Texas, we definitely recommend checking on rut dates for the area you are hunting on the Texas Parks and Wildlife website.

PHYSICAL CHARACTERISTICS

Body size varies greatly from the huge-bodied northern bucks to the South Texas body sizes, following Bergmann's Rule that the farther from the equator the larger the body size. But one thing is true for all South Central Plains bucks: they are capable of growing antlers that are second-to-none because of the highly fertile ground on which they live. Smaller in body size than their northern relatives, they often qualify for the record book because of their larger antler size and mass. "Age = Monster Bucks" is the equation in this area; no matter what math class you've ever taken. Hunters and landowners here have increased buck populations and decreased doe-to-buck ratios over the years, so many bucks are seen on most days of hunting, with ample opportunity to harvest mature bucks.

wife Kandi and son Kaleb, live in Iowa and have made a name for themselves filming huge bucks hitting the dirt. His penchant for filming has led Don to develop a hunting method that is still evolving. "Although I love to hunt from treestands, I've started to hunt from ground blinds a lot. We brush them in to standing corn in our food plots on land that we own or lease. A lot of the plots are three or four acres and we very meticulously brush a blind in at the edge of the corn. We did this originally because suitable stand trees were hard to find and we needed good footage.

"We then realized that we could use the corn behind the blind as an effective way into and out of the blinds. Now, we put a blind on each end of the cornfield to hunt different winds and we wait until the right chance to sneak out. If we do it right we don't blow out our fields, ever. Because of that we don't burn out our best spots."

Kisky prefers to put his blinds in early and leave them throughout the season, which is good advice for anyone using ground blinds for whitetails. If you don't have acres of food plots to work with, you can still use Kisky's strategy. Leased land or private land where you've secured permission might allow you the opportunity to brush-

Iowa is the go-to big-buck destination. Hunters often have to wait three years to draw a tag in this mecca of Booners.

HUNTER BIO | DON KISKY

AGE/HOMETOWN: 47/Hamilton, Mo.

YEARS HUNTING: 40 years

FAVORITE HUNT LOCATION:
Iowa and Canada

DEER HARVESTED:
Hundreds of does and around 90 bucks.

LARGEST BUCK: 213½ inches nontypical, 220 pounds live weight.

FAVORITE METHOD:
Grunting and rattling.

CONTACT INFO:
www.whitetailfreaks.com
www.facebook.com/whitetailfreakstv
www.twitter.com/whitetailfreaks
Whitetail Freaks on Outdoor Channel.

WHITETAIL SLAM: No

Texas makes up a large part of the South-Central Plains territory and is recognized as the state with the largest whitetail population – over 4 million animals.

ISTOCK

Kandi Kisky is shown here with a great whitetail taken in the South-Central Plains Region.

in a corn blind. Of course, you don't need corn. Hunters have started to use ground blinds in more situations as they realize that as long as they are brushed-in and seasoned, the deer will eventually accept them as part of the landscape.

If you're traveling to a new spot and plan to use a ground blind it's obviously going to be very tough to "season" your blind. This necessitates a serious brushing-in session, and while you're making your blind disappear, it pays to remember your scent. Rubber boots and rubber gloves sprayed down with a scent eliminator are a good idea. This might not be enough to fool all of the deer, but you just might fool the right one.

To brush-in his blinds, whether he's on his own farm or traveling, Kisky has a few tips, "I always use the natural habitat. You can use zip ties to secure brush to your blind but bailing twine works better. I also always make sure to stake down my blind, even if the forecast doesn't call for strong winds in the immediate future. Lastly, one of the most common mistakes I see is that hunters open their shooting ports or windows way too wide. You've got to keep it dark in the blind and that means narrow shooting ports."

MAKE SOME NOISE

No hunter should dare visit Missouri, Iowa, Texas or even Nebraska without a good set of rattling antlers. Few regions feature as callable deer as the South Central Plains. This is one of the reasons why hunting celebrity and wildlife biologist Larry Weishuhn spends so much time hunting these deer.

"My go-to tactic is always rattling horns, followed by a good shooting rest. I learned a long time ago through my research at Texas A&M with penned deer that they actually make all kinds of noises and are very vocal. I've used that to my advantage ever since, and I absolutely love to rattle.

"If it's early season I may not rattle as much, but might spend more time rubbing brush with the antlers. As it gets closer to the rut I'll try to mimic some sparring, with a mix of grunting tossed in. I'm just trying to

TOM MIRANDA

HUNTING TIP:
FACE AWAY FROM THEIR APPROACH

If you compare the stand-hanging techniques of a newcomer to our sport versus someone who has hunted hard for years you might notice one glaring difference. The beginner will almost always face his stand in the exact direction he expects the deer to approach from. The thought is that you can see them coming and get ready. The seasoned hunter might very well hang his stand 180 degrees around the same tree. This keeps you well hidden from approaching deer, and gives you the best chance to get into position for a broadside or quartering away shot once the deer is already past your tree. Typically, the deer will focus its attention on what is ahead of it, giving you the best chance to shoot as it passes your site.

KANDI KISKY

Kandi and Kaleb Kisky are shown here with two good reasons why the South-Central Plains is such a destination for whitetail hunters.

Many bucks are patterned on water in the South-Central Plains.

mimic two bucks pushing one another back and forth, not all out trying to kill each other. When it gets into the rut, though, the fights become much more serious and that's what I try to sound like.

"I've witnessed actual buck fights that lasted a couple of seconds, and some that were absolute battles that lasted eight hours and the bucks were breathing out of their mouths and totally worn out. Many times I'll incorporate snort-wheezing into my rattling sequences when bucks are really getting after it. There's nothing better than a big buck charging in to your set to kick some butt."

Catering rattling and calling sequences to the phase of the rut is a key piece of the equation. If you're out there in the beginning of October banging your antlers together as hard as possible, it's not likely you're going to get a positive response. The same goes for using estrus scents well outside of the rut or posturing decoys at the wrong time. Understanding what the deer expect to be happening in specific parts of the season is huge.

Although Weishuhn loves to rattle, he doesn't just show up at different places blindly hoping the deer will like the sounds of calls. He thoroughly researches certain areas before ever traveling to hunt to ensure he

Huntress Larysa Switlyk poses with a great Texas whitetail.

LARYSA SWITLYK

has a higher chance of running into a mature buck. "I always do my homework, regardless of whether I'm hunting Oklahoma, Texas or wherever. I call local game departments to find out about the age structure. I hunt for mature bucks and I want to hunt areas where at least 20 percent of the population is mature bucks. I also research deer density, buck-to-doe ratios and fawn crops.

"Few of us think about this, but if you want lots of four- or five-year-old bucks, you had better find out what the fawn crop was like four or five years ago. If there was some weather event, heavy predation, or some other factor that killed a high number of fawns, that's going to result in a gap in the age class you're looking for."

This may seem like information that's not available to the average hunter, but in this age of free information it is. Most state game agencies will have population estimates, fawn recruitment studies and harvest data readily available on their websites. If not, a quick call to the big-game biologist should provide you with plenty of information and a good jumping-off point to start your localized research.

NATHAN MRNAK

Nathan Mrnak devotes a lot of his time to on-the-ground scouting in the spring, and then employs multiple trail cameras throughout the summer to figure out what makes bucks like this Missouri monster tick.

YEAR-ROUND PURSUIT

A lot of the information on hunting the South-Central Plains Region comes from hunters visiting highly controlled properties where hunting pressure is nearly nonexistent and the deer are allowed to grow old. If that has you sour on the region, consider that there are

HUNTER BIO NATHAN MRNAK

NATHAN MRNAK

AGE/HOMETOWN: 36/Park Rapids, Minn.

YEARS HUNTING: 26 years

FAVORITE HUNT LOCATION: South-Central Plains Region and northern Missouri.

DEER HARVESTED: Over 80

LARGEST BUCK: 176 inches, 250 pounds.

FAVORITE METHOD: Archery from treestands.

CONTACT INFO: Cabela's Outdoor Adventures, www.cabelasoutdooradventures.com.

WHITETAIL SLAM: Yes, an archery SLAM, and one buck shy of a gun SLAM.

WINDIGO IMAGES

CRUSHING THE LULL

Serious Midwestern buck hunters know all too well the difficulties of the October lull. It's a time when the weather and moon are seemingly perfect for deer movement – yet mature bucks appear to vanish. Day after day does and young bucks track by stand sets with hunters climbing down after dark empty-handed.

With mature deer resting up for the onset of the rut, nocturnal activity is the rule. Hunters who must score in the lull need to hunt tight in buck security cover and near bedding areas. The difficulty this time of year is the threat of spooking out target bucks by crowding in too close.

One strategy used by veteran buck killers during pre-rut and the October lull is known as bump and dump. In this scenario, the hunter walks into a known big buck hideout in midmorning and bumps the target buck from his bed. Immediately, the hunter sets up his stand and climbs in. The beauty of this strategy is that the mature buck isn't spooked by human odor in his travels yet, but is flushed out as if a farmer or woodcutter has invaded his area. Since mature deer are creatures of habit, the brute will likely return – usually later that same day – and may even attempt to lie in the same bed.

Typically hunters who locate mature bucks resist pressuring them, yet in the October lull big whitetails limit movement to a very small core area – maybe only a 50-yard circle of woods. Finding this "nest" can be tricky.

If you simply don't have the right setup or mindset to employ the bump-and-dump, consider rethinking your entire strategy. Part of the reason for the lull is that the food sources are changing. Crops are being harvested, acorns might be dropping or already eaten up, and much of the green browse is turning brown. Deer live off of their stomachs, so what many feel is a true lull is only partially a decrease in activity. The reality is that many of the deer have switched food sources and all of a sudden your field edge stands might go dead.

To combat this, consider going out with a climbing stand or a lightweight portable to observe new areas that you haven't hunted yet. This might be an oak ridge or a saddle well off of any field edge, or simply a wooded flat that offers good visibility. Always carry your binoculars and try to move to new spots until you pin down current deer movement.

Another possible way to beat the lull is to go out with the intention of filling a few antlerless tags. Shooting does during the first week or two of the season or during the rut can be a bad idea, but if you're deer activity has died during the middle of October, that might be a perfect time to fill the freezer with venison. This can be a lot of fun and it will keep you out there hunting, which is the only way you're going to kill a mature buck.

HUNTING TIP: TAKE A REST

If you decide to visit one of the many big-buck producing states that are nestled firmly in the South-Central Plains Region and you're going to tote a firearm, always pack some kind of rest. Some hunters prefer a monopod, while others opt for a bipod or tripod. Whatever you choose, make sure to shoot off of it before ever hitting the road to ensure that it works for your shooting style. Too many hunters feel like they can shoot offhand, especially when hunting from a treestand, but this is a bad idea. You don't want to have a Booner at the far end of your effective range only to realize your only option is to shoot offhand. If you have to, at the very least use a solid tree trunk or limb to keep yourself as steady as possible.

huge tracts of public land spread throughout the region. Many are in some places that you simply wouldn't expect like Kansas, Arkansas and even Texas, which has a reputation as being completely locked up by leases.

For the hunter looking to hunt these spots, or simply knock on a few doors for access to private land, the hunting will take on a different feel than on those highly regulated properties. For starters, you'll need to do more work than others, but that's okay, it's part of the fun. One hunter who fully engages in a year-round approach to whitetails is Nebraska's Nathan Mrnak.

Mrnak prides himself on scouting in the preseason to the point where he can get a good lead on a mature buck, and put himself in the best position to arrow that buck once the season opens. "Hunting simply doesn't start with the opener for me. I'm big on the preseason scouting. I use trail cameras, aerial photos and maps, but nothing beats boots on the ground.

"Because of this I spend a lot of time walking through my hunting areas in turkey season. Even if I'm actually turkey hunting or shed hunting, I'm always looking for the next best tree to hang a stand in. Those perfect trees, of course, need to be in a spot that already funnels deer movement for one reason or another. There's just something about finding the right spot with a good stand tree six months before the season that makes you feel like you've got a leg up on the deer. While I'm making those spring scouting forays I can still see old rubs and sometimes scrapes, so I have a good idea whether a mature buck was using that exact spot during the fall."

Mrnak's quest for the perfect treestand tree is important, because many hunters shed hunt or scout in the spring but they tend to look for the old sign without trying to identify the exact spot to kill a buck come fall. The best bet for this style of scouting is to carry surveyor tape or some other flagging tool so that you can mark the tree and come back to it at any time. It's too easy to believe that you'll remember the exact location of a tree you found in

March when you go to hang midsummer stands, but the woods will change considerably and you might not be able to locate the exact tree. That's an easy problem to avoid with some flagging tape.

Another common mistake spring scouters make is to look only for good rut stand sites. Mrnak sees this often, and advises against it. "It's not always about finding the best rut spots. There is nothing wrong with this, but to be a good hunter you also have to be able to kill them early and late in the season. You can't rely solely on the rut, especially if you're going to travel to a couple of different states.

"I sell hunting trips to hunters through my job with Cabela's and a lot of folks ask for the prime rut dates. I tell them to consider being the first to hunt with an outfitter or the first person on a tract of land. It's hard to consider a September or October hunt when you know things are going to be popping during November, but being the first person to hunt a spot has a lot of merit."

As the spring gives way to summer Mrnak starts to use a lot of trail cameras to try to pattern big bucks as they move through their environment. "You can be successful in the early season if you spend some time in the summer trying to pattern big bucks, but not just by seeing them come out into agricultural fields in the evenings. I want to know where his core area is and

KRIS SEYMOUR

Kansas buck hunter Kris Seymour shows off some whopper Prairie State antler drops. Looks like a target buck for the coming season.

HUNTER BIO | LARRY WEISHUHN

LARRY WEISHUHN

AGE/HOMETOWN: 65/Uvalde, Texas

YEARS HUNTING: 60 years

FAVORITE HUNT LOCATION:
South Texas brush country or Sonora, Mexico.

DEER HARVESTED: Over 2,500

LARGEST BUCK: 230 inches, 300 pounds.

FAVORITE METHOD: Rattling, calling, spot and stalk, and still-hunting.

CONTACT INFO:
Larry Weishuhn Outdoors on Facebook

Sportsman Channel TV show – *DSC's Trailing the Hunter's Moon*

Books: *Pear Flat Philosophies* - Safari Press
Hunting Mature Bucks - Krause Publication
Attracting Whitetails - Derrydale Press
Southern Deer & Deer Hunting - Krause Publication
Whitetails East & West - Stoeger Press
Trailing the Hunter's Moon - Stoeger Press

Blogs: NatureBlind.com, Ruger.com, ZeissHunting.com, Hornady.com

WHITETAIL SLAM: Yes, and nearly an Ultimate SLAM.

Hunt Master Gregg Ritz used his T/C muzzleloader to spank this Iowa bruiser at the Lakosky "Crush" property.

SHE Safari designer Pam Zaitz shows off a 200-inch whitetail taken in the South Texas brush country. Wow!

Minnesota's Melissa Bachman continues her quest for the Whitetail SLAM with this dandy Missouri archery buck.

how he travels to and from it. In September I hunt the fringes of bedding areas and try very hard to only hunt when the conditions are right. Everyone says the best time to hunt a stand is the first time you sit it, and that's right. If I've done my homework and I wait for ideal conditions I feel like I up my odds of killing a particular buck. It doesn't always work, but sometimes it does and that's good enough for me."

Mrnak's strategy for hunting the fringes of bedding areas is a good one but requires attention to detail on scent control and overall intrusion. Because you're planning to get close to a big buck's core area, it's necessary to be extremely cautious about wind, and entrance and exit routes. A lot of hunters avoid hunting close to bedding areas because of the chance of spooking the deer. In many places, especially areas with a decent amount of hunting pressure, this is one of the best ways to kill older bucks – simply because you put yourself in a position to catch a mature deer on his feet during daylight.

LICENSE OPPORTUNITIES

A lot of the pressure from traveling hunters in the South-Central Plains Region involves bowhunters. Bowhunters fill up outfitting operations regularly during the early season and the rut, and that puts a premium on available lands, which often creates the perception that you have to be a bowhunter to get a tag in certain states. This is simply not true.

Nonresident firearms hunters in many of the premier states can still get tags, and a few states like Iowa oftentimes have a shorter wait for drawing a tag than their bowhunting counterparts. Some states are restrictive on their firearms tags, while others are wide open. A few even offer over-the-counter muzzleloader licenses, which can be a great way to kill a large buck when the snow is falling. Research into the availability of tags can go a long way toward making a hunt happen.

If you live outside of the South-Central Plains Region, consider hitting the road at some point to hunt this territory. Depending on just where you decide to hunt, you're likely to run into just about every type of cover that whitetails live in. If you time your hunt around the rut you might experience deer hunting as everyone should at least once in their lifetime. If you go in the early or late season, you might miss the crowds and still wrap your tag around the largest buck of your life. Certainly, any SLAM-minded individuals out there owe it to themselves to visit this region, if for nothing other than the best chance at a buck sporting antlers of epic proportions.

CHAPTER 10

NORTHWESTERN

(Odocoileus virginianus leucurus and Odocoileus virginianus ochrourus)

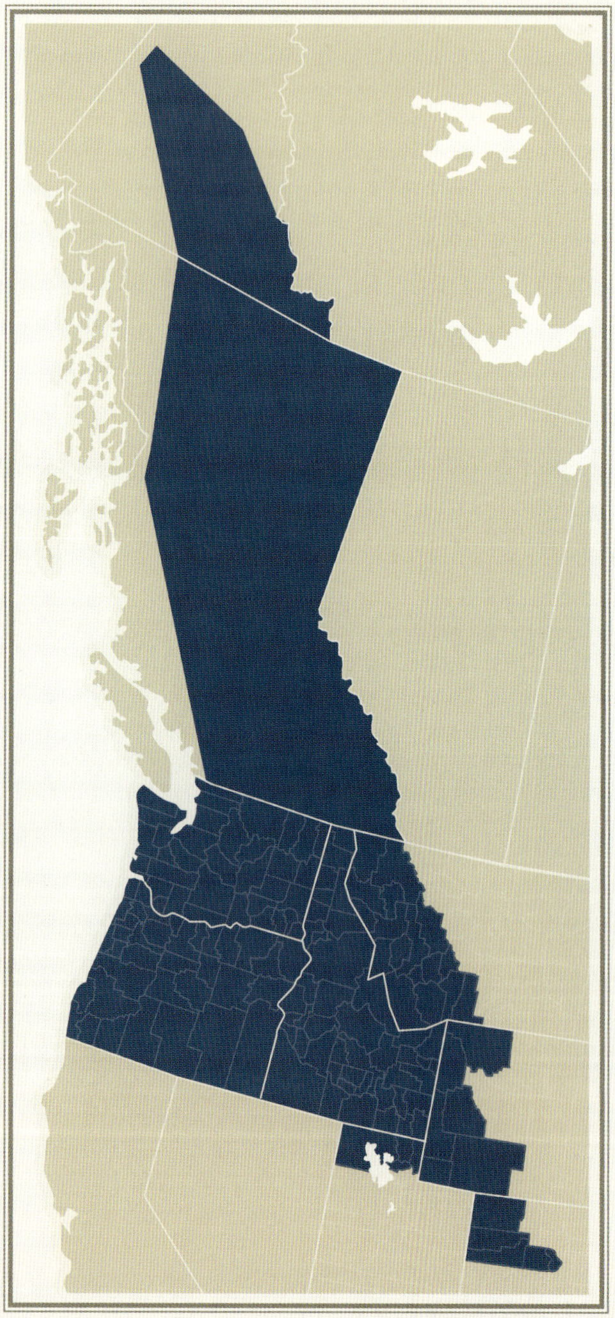

Most hunters who head out to the Northwestern Region of the whitetail's range probably have elk, mule deer and maybe even sheep or mountain goats on their minds – but not whitetails. The American Northwest is home to a diverse variety of game animals, and although there are some huge whitetails in the region, they're definitely a somewhat ignored resource, which is good news for any hunter willing to travel to the area.

If you're among that select group, don't expect a typical Midwestern-style whitetail hunt. Certainly you can kill a mature buck on the edge of an agricultural field as he feeds contentedly, but you also might find yourself hunting deer at elevations that don't exist in the Midwest. You may find buck rubs and scrapes in places that look like they should host bugling bull elk instead of grunting whitetail bucks. Many of the deer in this region are living proof of the adaptability of whitetails, and it's quite likely that you'll agree as soon as your lungs and legs start burning from the climb up to your stand.

Not all of the deer in this territory require an ascent though, many still call the lower elevations home and just like the Dakota Region, river bottoms are often teeming with deer herds. A good mix of public and private land will greet the traveling hunter and if you're willing to do a little research and a lot of work, you can tag a great Northwestern whitetail.

Interested hunters might also notice that the Northwestern Region covers a tremendous distance when measured from the southern tip, which dips into Colorado, all the way through British Columbia north into the Yukon Territories of Canada. If you're looking for diversity in a region, look no further than here.

The rut in the Pacific Northwest looks like the rut anywhere else and is just as exciting to hunt.

ALL ABOUT THE NORTHWESTERN DEER

BY DR. HARRY JACOBSON

RANGE

Two subspecies of whitetails are present in the Northwestern Region of the Whitetail SLAM.

O.v. leucurus, commonly called the "Columbia Whitetail," is the westernmost representative of all whitetails, and was first documented in 1829 by explorer David Douglas along the Cowlitz and Willamette Rivers. Back then the subspecies was found as far north as Olympia, Wash., east to The Dalles, Ore., and west to the mouth of the Columbia River. Habitat loss, unregulated hunting and outright poaching led to decline, and in 1978 they were placed on the U.S. endangered species list.

Protection and sound management over several decades has led to a population recovery, and this coveted deer was delisted as an endangered species in 2003. Today more than 6,000 Columbia whitetails call Oregon's Umpqua River valley home. Approximately 800 deer are in the lower Columbia drainage, and a thriving population of approximately 6,400 animals lives in Douglas County. Hunting reopened in 2005 with 23 permits available in the public drawing, and 110 going directly to landowners, as most of the hunting available was on private land. In 2010 Oregon issued 146 permits in the public drawing and 54 private land permits.

O.v. ochrourus, commonly called the "Idaho" or "Northwestern" whitetail, is found in the northern U.S. Rockies (Montana, Wyoming, Idaho, Oregon and Washington), and Alberta and British Columbia of western Canada. Noted for their dark color and robust size, these high-plains deer can also be found at midlevel elevations to above 6,000 feet in mountain ranges. Sightings have occurred as far north as the southern areas of the Northwest Territories, but the vast majority are found in Alberta and southern British Columbia, making this animal one of the northernmost dwelling of all deer.

PHYSICAL CHARACTERISTICS

The Columbia has smaller antlers and bodies than many of its cousins. A 140-inch Boone and Crockett buck is a really nice trophy, although some can reach up to 160 inches. Unfortunately, the subspecies is not currently recognized by either B&C or Safari Club International, so any trophies taken are not likely to score well. But many people are lobbying for its recognition and we hope it will be included soon.

RUT TIMING

Peak breeding times occur from Nov. 10 – Thanksgiving in Washington and Oregon. Peak rut timing throughout the Rockies is generally accepted as the last two weeks of November.

ANCESTRY

In chapter one, Dr. James Kroll discussed the likelihood that white-tailed deer are descendants of black-tailed deer. With the Pacific Northwest the home of California and Columbia blacktails, hunting the Northwestern whitetail subgroup makes for an interesting proposition. Blacktail bucks have often been known to spend summers at elevation in bachelor herds where breezes keep temperatures cooler and insects at a minimum. As the rut approaches, these bucks migrate to lower elevations in search of the estrus does which live in the river bottoms and swamp thickets.

Columbia whitetails exhibit this same behavior, and hunters in pursuit of these deer often see only does and young bucks until the mature bucks move to the lowlands for breeding. Wet conditions dominate the rut season in the coastal Northwest, which can make these hunts miserable.

Hunters traveling to the Northwestern Region should consider sighting their rifles in for longer shot distances than they are accustomed to in their local hunting areas.

TONY PETERSON

The Northwestern territory offers hunters a chance to hunt multiple species like elk and mule deer along with whitetails. A Polaris Ranger helps access remote country.

Cross the Cascade Mountains to the east and you will notice that the habitat changes greatly. Here Northwestern whitetails live in irrigated farm country reminiscent of the Midwest. Crop fields break up the timber and deer key in on a bounty of fresh grain and orchard fruit.

WESTERN TACTICS

Few hunters are as familiar with the Northwestern deer as Steve West, who owns Steve's Outdoor Adventures, a top-notch booking agency for hunters looking to link up with outfitters. West lives in Oregon and hunts the region each fall, but he doesn't necessarily follow the typical whitetail hunter's playbook.

"I'm a western big-game hunter at heart, so you're not likely to catch me sitting in treestands. I don't grow food plots or pattern whitetails either, at least not the way most hunters do. I prefer to hunt whitetails like mule deer by glassing from long distances and then plan a stalk. This might involve sitting two miles away from an alfalfa field or a mountainside slowly picking

HUNTING TIP: LONG RANGE WEAPONRY

A hunter in northern Michigan would probably never consider a 400- or 500-yard rifle shot, but that might be what it takes to kill a whitetail in the Northwestern Region. If you plan to hunt the territory, consider practicing at farther distances than you'd consider on your home turf. There is nothing that says you have to take a poke at such distance, but being able to shoot farther might mean the difference between backstraps and tag soup. This goes for bowhunters as well. The average shot distances in much of the whitetail's range may be around 20 yards, but you can double that when you start heading west. Modern bows, rifles and muzzleloaders are all capable of handling longer shots, but it's up to the individual to ensure that they are fully ready and confident to take a longer shot should the situation arise.

A snow camo cover-up comes in handy not only on snowy days but when tree canopies are bare of leaves.

TOM MIRANDA

ISTOCK

Many areas of the Northwestern Region offer the chance to engage in long-distance glassing to find gagger bucks like this mature whitetail.

apart cover until I see a buck worth trying to stalk."

West's methods of locating deer require optics not often found in the whitetail world. To spot distant deer and judge racks from more than a mile away means spotting scopes with serious magnification paired with a quality, hunter-friendly tripod. Too many hunters buy an expensive spotting scope and then go cheap with the tripod, but that's a major mistake. Jerky movements and difficulty slowly scanning or zooming in on a deer can be frustrating and lead to a lost opportunity. Find a spotting scope tripod that allows for minute adjustments and ease of operation, without worrying about bulk and weight.

When West locks onto a potential target buck he doesn't rush in, which is a common mistake. "I never try to push the envelope with a whitetail buck. I'll watch an individual deer to see how he is moving and bedding. Whenever I'm watching a buck that I want to eventually stalk, I always pay attention to the wind, which is difficult from two miles away. I take note of the way the stalks of grass or treetops are moving, and how the buck relates to that wind movement. Deer live off of their noses and I know that if a buck beds on a certain bench or ridge when the wind is blowing from

DUAL-PURPOSE TRIPS

Since the Northwestern Region is a destination for hunters with a wide variety of game animals on their minds, consider how you could incorporate whitetails into a different hunt to the region. If you're heading out to elk hunt for example, it might be a good idea to spend a day scouting some deer-friendly mountain lowlands during your trip. This is extremely hard to do when you've got an elk tag in your pocket, but what you find might prompt you to return with a deer tag.

If carving time out of a fall hunt is too much, consider a spring turkey or bear trip to the region. You might stumble across some shed antlers or witness a greening alfalfa field that is teeming with spring deer. These trips can be invaluable should you decide to revisit the area in search of a SLAM buck.

Other options include a fishing trip or family vacation that involves a bit of on-the-ground whitetail scouting. Deer leave a lot of sign and are highly visible in the spring and summer. Any whitetail hunter worth their salt in the woods should be able to devote a small amount of time to identifying potential hunting hotspots. Once identified, Internet research can be used to fine-tune locations and plan for an all-out deer hunting trip.

If you embark on a guided hunt in the Northwest, ask your outfitter about whitetail hunting. Even if he doesn't personally guide for deer, he will likely know someone who does and can turn you on to a good operation.

the north, he will probably do the same thing again when the wind is out of the same direction. This is very important for planning my stalk."

It's easy to understand how mule deer bed and move in relation to wind direction, but it's not easy with whitetails because in most of their range they just aren't that visible. This doesn't mean that hunters in the Midwest and East can't use this information to their advantage though. One way to pin down when a buck is likely to move is to use trail cameras and then document what direction the wind was blowing when you got images of a buck traveling. This will key you in to individual deer preferences and can lead to higher hunting success.

Once West has studied a particular buck through his spotting scope he'll try to note any other nontarget deer in the area. "In my opinion, whitetails are more alert than mule deer. Unseen bedded does are a stalk killer and they don't just get up and run off like muley does will. Whitetail does will get up and snort until they alert every deer in the area. I always try to find a loner buck or at least plan a stalk around any does that might be bedded close.

"One thing that helps me accomplish this is by watch-

DENNIS CAMPBELL

Here a young Dennis Campbell shows off an Idaho mountain whitetail.

HUNTER BIO STEVE WEST

STEVE WEST

AGE/HOMETOWN: La Grande, Ore.

YEARS HUNTING: 15 years

FAVORITE HUNT LOCATION:
Sheridan, Wyo. – the eastern slope and foothills of the Bighorn Mountains.

DEER HARVESTED: 23 whitetail bucks.

LARGEST BUCK: 161 inches gross Boone and Crockett – 11 pointer.

FAVORITE METHOD:
Western-style spot and stalk.

CONTACT INFO:
www.stevesoutdooradventures.com or
www.steveshunts.com
Our office number is 1-800-303-1304.

WHITETAIL SLAM: No, I am missing two.

Few regions of the Whitetail SLAM can rival the sheer beauty that the Northwestern Region offers.

TOM MIRANDA

HUNTING TIP: SLEEPER STATES

Read about sleeper whitetail states and you're likely to hear about Nebraska, Oklahoma or Kentucky. No doubt, these states are producing great bucks and offer opportunities for the traveling hunter, but what about Oregon or Washington? Both are extremely underrated for big whitetails, partially because of the availability of game like Roosevelt elk and other more desirable species. This leaves the whitetail hunter free to chase relatively lightly pressured deer in these states – not to mention Idaho, which is a top elk hunting destination. Idaho may be the best big-buck state you've never considered. An open mind can go a long way toward filling a tag on a bruiser buck in the Northwestern Region.

DENNIS CAMPBELL

Alabama big-game hunter Dennis Campbell took this tough-to-hunt Columbia whitetail. Columbia whitetails are a separate subspecies but classified as Northwestern in the Whitetail SLAM.

TOM MIRANDA

Fall snowstorms in mountain country move deer and make hunting tough.

ing for the thermals to kick in during the evening. In the mountains the thermals are very pronounced and reliable, so once I see that the air is rushing down the mountains in the early evening I know that's not likely to change during my stalk."

This puts West in a position to solidify his stalking plan and engage it. Whitetail hunters everywhere can use thermals to their advantage, just as they can get busted by the rising morning air or sinking evening air. Deer are very tuned-in to thermals and will travel and bed accordingly.

Because of this, West has to be very careful about the last leg of his stalk as he tries to ease into muzzleloader or rifle range. "Mountain deer are like sheep in that they bed in places where they can see everything approaching below them and smell everything above them. In mountain country you have to stay back and watch them, and then figure out how to get out of sight and above them. Once you successfully get above them, you've nearly won. They just don't expect danger to come from above so they don't spend a lot of time looking uphill. This is the key to finishing a stalk and killing them in their beds, or as they get up from their beds."

RIVER BOTTOMS

Typically bowhunters ambush western deer from a treestand nestled in a giant cottonwood tree. Images of Montana's Milk River or the Big Sioux River of South Dakota come to mind. In the Northwest subgroup

Ohio hunter Adam Hays with his Northwestern bow buck.

these same tactics play out in eastern Washington and Oregon. Often the only dense security cover is found along the ribbons of rivers winding through the flat country. Mornings are spent glassing bucks from a distance as they leave crop fields and travel into river-bottom cover. Stands are set for evening hunts to ambush bucks returning – hopefully on the same trails. This game of cat and mouse sounds like a sure thing but often bucks follow a pattern of browsing up or down the river. Then they pop out either in another field, or at the very least on a trail out of range.

Some creative hunters will use a boat or hip boots to cross shallow rivers to access bedding area stands for morning hunts, but typically these river-bottom bucks are hunted during afternoon sits. During the rut these river stands can be sat in all day, and if a hunter can plan the set to utilize prevailing winds to blow human scent out over the water, this can be a huge advantage. Stand trees right on the river bank can make great rattling positions as bucks that answer the call are prevented from circling downwind by the river barrier.

AMBUSHING NORTHWESTERNS

While West is much more apt to stalk a whitetail than try to ambush one, he is not above the method. "I was hunting Montana with Phil Phillips one time and we were glassing an alfalfa field when we spotted two giant whitetails walking through a notch in a monster rock wall. They then crossed a flooded field and went into some cottonwoods along the Bighorn River. I said right then and there that I was going to go after them and try to pin them against the river and shoot the biggest buck.

"Phil talked me out of that plan by insisting that you can't pin a whitetail down with a river and that I'd blow the whole bottom out when I tried. He sug-

WINDIGO IMAGES

Hunting whitetails in the mountains was once unheard of… yet whitetails continue to expand their range.

gested we climb into a spot above the notch and wait for the bucks to come back through. I've got the attention span of a three-year-old on speed, so I didn't want to do this, but I followed his advice. As the night progressed I wanted to strangle Phil – and then we saw a giant buck chasing does. He was grunting all over and all-of-a-sudden he started our way. I learned a valuable lesson there."

These situations happen countless times to hunters across the country. What you think you know can sometimes be your worst enemy during a whitetail hunt, especially when conditions dictate a tactic that isn't in your wheelhouse. This is also a good reminder that just because a tactic is very common in a certain region, that doesn't mean it's the only means to an end.

West is a self-admitted stalking junkie who doesn't prefer to pattern deer in the traditional sense. That doesn't mean hunters with plenty of scouting time can't dial in the daily movements of a good Northwestern buck. In fact, the visibility of deer in the region, which benefits spot-and-stalk hunters, benefits sit-and-wait hunters as well.

CHAPTER 11

DESERT WHITETAIL

(Odocoileus virginianus couesi)

Hunting desert Coues deer requires lots of glassing.

TOM MIRANDA

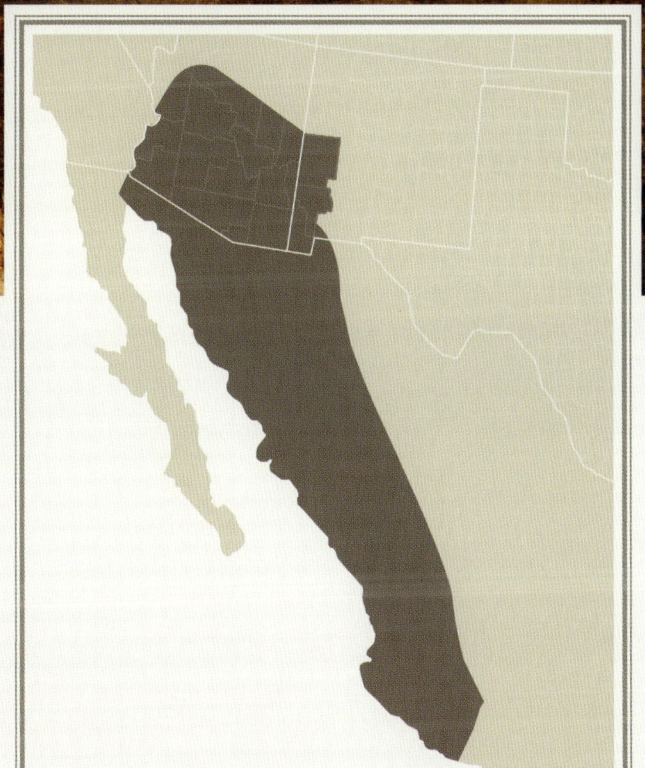

Even the most heavily pressured deer on the East Coast pale in comparison to Coues deer when it comes to sheer environmental awareness and neurotic focus on avoiding predators of all shapes and sizes. The diminutive Coues has grown immensely popular over the last two decades as more and more devout whitetailers have become aware of the hunting opportunities, and the pure challenge of taking a Coues deer with any weapon.

The challenge not only lies in the very nature of Coues deer, who spend a fair amount of their lives avoiding mountain lions, but also in the terrain they occupy. Deserts, while beautiful in their own distant way, are unforgiving to say the least. To sidestep cactus all day long and glass a brown and gray world while trying to pick out a small, brown deer that has evolved perfectly for its surroundings is no easy task. Add in the fact that while you can find lone bucks on occasion, most of the time a Coues deer will have company, which compounds the amount of eyes, ears and noses you need to contend with; you'll realize where the Desert whitetail gets its reputation.

You can employ varying tactics to take your Coues and certainly not be locked in to spotting and stalking them. Every year hunters fill their tags by ambushing them as they travel throughout their home ranges. Adding a Desert whitetail to your SLAM is a worthy goal of any hunter who fancies himself a true student of all-things-deer. One such hunter, Oklahoma resident Eddie Claypool, has been traveling west in search of bowhunting adventure in the desert for over 20 years, and he has boiled Coues deer hunting down to a science.

WHERE TO START?

Of his beginnings in the Coues deer quest, Claypool remembers well his initial planning. "The first year was 1994 and I just decided to give Coues deer a try, so I called a biologist in Arizona and chatted with him about areas to hunt. I loaded my truck and drove to the southeast part of Arizona, and then pretty much toured through the available ground in New Mexico too. I was just trying to figure out where they lived."

Claypool has been at the do-it-yourself hunting game for his entire life, and the willingness to figure out what animals are prone to do in a new area is one of the cornerstones of his success. Traveling in search of deer – in any region on your own – will almost certainly subject you to a learning curve that you've long forgotten on your home hunting ground. But, paying close attention to habitat, sign and deer sightings will

Coues deer are regarded as the toughest of all whitetails to kill. Nothing can compare to these tiny desert dwellers when it comes to situational awareness.

ISTOCK

ALL ABOUT THE DESERT WHITETAIL

BY DR. HARRY JACOBSON

RANGE

Coues deer (properly pronounced "cows", but nearly everyone says "coos") are commonly known as the "Arizona whitetail." The core of the Coues deer range is in southeastern Arizona where there are vast areas of Forest Service and BLM land. Coues deer are also found in New Mexico and Mexico. This deer has developed such a reputation for being able to vanish from view in the smallest amount of cover that it is frequently referred to as the "gray ghost."

RUT TIMING

The prime Coues deer rut occurs throughout the month of January, although rutting activity can still be witnessed as early as the first week of December. This typically signifies the pre-rut, with the main chasing and breeding occurring throughout January. Hunters would be wise to plan their hunt around the Coues deer rut because it brings out the biggest and most mature deer.

PHYSICAL CHARACTERISTICS

Adaptation to the desert habitat has made Coues deer one of the smallest deer in North America, measuring just 28 to 32 inches at the shoulder and about 56 inches from head to tail. Large bucks tip the scales at 80 to 90 pounds, with mature does weighing about 65 pounds. Despite their tiny body size, Coues can carry proportionally impressive antlers. However, to meet Boone and Crockett record book status antlers are still considerably smaller than all other white-tailed deer. Currently, to make the all-time record book, a Coues whitetail needs to score 110 typical, or 120 nontypical. All other whitetails recognized by Boone and Crockett need to score 170 typical or 195 nontypical.

expedite the learning process and put you in a better position to fill a tag.

"During that first trip I settled into some mountain foothills on a huge piece of public land. I chose a site for my base camp and just started scouting on foot, with the mindset that I needed to look at new ground every single day until I figured something out. It was a new experience hiking into the manzanita, oaks and desert mesquite looking for any sign of Coues deer.

"As I began to find a few deer I started to spot-and-stalk them, but it quickly became apparent that I was going to have a tough row to hoe in that department. Sneaking up on them was a losing battle for me and even when I did get into range I had a hard time getting off a shot given the terrain. It was frustrating, however, I started finding rubs, scrapes and well-used trails and I started to wonder if I couldn't hunt them like the whitetails in the Midwest. I began sitting only 10 or 12 feet up in some of the oaks, because that is as high as you can get, and I actually started having a few

Most Coues hunters look for bucks in the rocky relief of mountainsides. Glass the lower third of the mountain as mountain lions often are found higher.

TOM MIRANDA

encounters."

Forcing a tactic of any sort is a hunt-killer as Claypool demonstrated with his early forays into Coues deer country. This is extremely common with traveling hunters who live off the tactics they use for success at home. It's crucial to remember that deer of all subspecies vary greatly in their willingness to play the game your way, and a buck in one region might not care one whit about your rattling sequence – while a buck 1,000 miles away in a different region might charge in with complete reckless abandonment.

Then of course, there are the variances between individual deer, environmental influences, season timing, hunting pressure, and a host of other factors that influence how to hunt a specific spot. Pay attention to your instincts and keep an open mind and you'll find yourself adapting much better to the challenge of traveling to hunt. Better yet – you'll be more successful.

Once Claypool decided to hunt deer his way by climbing into a tree and waiting them out he realized a few things. "Sitting in a tree in the desert is boring, really boring. You need to have the patience of Job. That

A spotting scope can be an awesome whitetail hunting aide. So can a quiet ATV.

Stalking Coues deer is tough. Not only are they spooky, but the low vegetation of the desert hides interference animals and typically the stalk is over before the bowhunter gets in range.

TOM MIRANDA

TOM MIRANDA

Here Tom Miranda's 10-point Coues buck drinks while Tom sits at full draw.

first time I hunted them I settled on a little area that had a decent population of Coues deer, and on the last night I climbed a mountain bench and got into a tree. For five hours I watched nothing much happen, but as dusk settled in I witnessed a good buck easing along a trail. I made the shot with only a few minutes to spare and after the recovery I eventually realized he was a good one. In fact, at the time he was the number-three bow kill in the world and is still my best Coues buck."

STARTING OVER, EVERY YEAR

Although this is a general statement that is certain to warrant many exceptions, eastern whitetails are fairly reliable from year to year. If you've got a good funnel, pinch point, or bedding area, each will likely produce deer sightings annually. Food sources will change and hunting pressure might put the deer down some, but for the most part the deer will use the terrain and travel routes the same way from year to year. Not so much with Coues deer, as Claypool explains, "It's so frustrating, but Coues deer just seem to float around from spot to spot, area to area.

"Even in the areas that I know well it's always a chore to find the deer when I show up fresh. I don't know what exactly drives them from one place to the next but I have to guess that it could be drought, but is more likely due to mountain lions. However, even saying that I know how dependent on water sources Coues deer are. It's a toss-up, but I know that no matter what moves them, something always seems to. That means I always plan to put my boots to the ground every year when I go Coues deer hunting until I find a concentration of them that I'm comfortable hunting."

TOM MIRANDA

Deer tend to drink every day, which means as a bowhunter, finding water is like finding gold in the desert.

DOE-GROUP JACKPOT

Although you can hunt Coues deer in the early season, Claypool opts for later in the season when they are rutting, usually in January. The reasons for that are threefold, with the first being that the weather will be much more tolerable. The second is that January weather puts down the snakes, scorpions and other nasty desert-dwellers making the entire trip much safer. Lastly, hunting during the rut gets the bucks on their feet and ensures Claypool will have a much better chance of ambushing a buck as it covers ground in search of doe groups. If Claypool has done his homework correctly, he'll be around doe groups.

"I like to find hotspots where there is a doe group. Usually this is indicated by fresh rubs and scrapes, and in some situations the area will just be tore up with buck sign. Once I find this I try really hard to scout the area extensively and identify a few spots where the bucks are most likely to travel. Just like eastern whitetails, the Coues rut is crazy and subordinate bucks will cruise all over, but mature bucks are much more likely to sit on a group of does and wait them out. In between are the middle-aged bucks that score well and travel a lot, and those are the ones you're most likely to kill. Either way, I'll sit on a doe group all day long once I identify a good area and a few key ambush spots. That's important for Coues because it doesn't seem like first and last light are nearly as important to movement, meaning they move all day long. This is probably because they live in such big country and are so confident in their ability to stay hidden."

Sitting all day long staring at a seemingly sterile land is not for everyone, but Claypool's record has proven that it is a great method for tagging out on big Coues deer, especially if you shirk the guidance of an outfitter and opt for an on-your-own hunt on public land.

TURN A BLIND EYE

Ground blinds can also be used effectively in Coues country. Hidden blinds that guard active water holes or stock tanks can be dynamite. Coues bucks will often drink during midday – especially when rut chasing is in full swing. Desert hunters know that shade is a premium, and locating canvas hides under mesquite or ironwood trees that cast cool shade and block the hot southwestern sun is crucial.

One sneaky trait of Coues bucks is that at the water hole they will bend over to drink and then suddenly raise their head quickly at full alert. It's as if the buck is offering a bluff drink and is ready to spring away at the slightest sound or movement. Bowhunters who have gotten to full draw before the buck is at the water often shoot at this opportunity and consequently make a bad hit on a jumpy buck. Once the deer feels that all is okay he will settle down and begin a full 30-second drink. This behavior is very similar to African plains game. Smart bowhunters allow the animal to relax and

TOM MIRANDA

Reading in a ground blind helps pass slow times – but don't get too wrapped up in the book as Coues bucks can easily sneak into range.

Tom Miranda's 10-point Desert whitetail. Only about 5 percent of mature Coues bucks carry a 10-point frame, most are six or eight pointers.

drink before centering pins on vitals and touching the release.

Choose a ground blind that offers plenty of room and the ability to remain undetected. This might necessitate choosing a blind that features mesh window coverings. Instead of having an open shooting port that might give the deer a better chance of picking out movement, mesh coverings allow you the chance to have more open viewing, but remain hidden. If you do opt for this choice, make sure you spend time practicing shooting through the mesh before you go on the hunt. Some broadheads, especially mechanical or expandable heads, will open up when they pass through mesh. Figure this out long before the hunt to know

Pictured here is a giant Coues deer that Eddie Claypool killed during a DIY trip in 1994. The buck gross scored a shade over 108 inches!

EDDIE CLAYPOOL

that your hard-won shot won't stick into the dirt seven feet in front of your buck because of premature blade deployment.

Another ground blind consideration is noise. Some blinds, especially inexpensive ones, are noisier to set up and use. Take note of the window coverings, shooting ports and zippers. If any of these seem loud to operate while you set the blind up in your yard, they will seem deafening when actually hunting Coues deer.

In consideration of other game-spooking noise, it's a good idea to silence your bow in every way possible. From in-the-string silencers to a vibration-dampening stabilizer, make sure that every possible piece of your bow that could create unnecessary noise and vibration simply won't. This includes adding felt or moleskin to your rest launcher arm. Coues deer that seem to be completely at ease can duck the string at the shot, and since they are such small targets to begin with, a drop of three or four inches can mean the difference between a vital hit and a complete miss.

If you plan to spend your time hunting from a ground blind one thing worth considering, especially if your hunt will occur around the rut, is to try to rattle. Coues bucks will fight and establish territory just like eastern whitetails, and occasionally you can call them in by mimicking two bucks taking their aggression out on one another.

This is a great method to try periodically when the action has slowed down and you're staring at your watch. Just make sure that there aren't any visible deer nearby because a sudden fight erupting next to them will certainly send them scurrying through the brush. Give a quick scan of the surrounding area with your binoculars to ensure the coast is clear, and then rattle much like you would for an eastern whitetail. You just might be surprised at how a wily Coues buck will throw caution to the wind to check out who is banging heads in his territory.

A RESIDENT'S PERSPECTIVE

John Stallone is a Coues deer hunting fool who just happens to call Scottsdale, Ariz., home. Living in the heart of Desert whitetail country has provided Stallone with the perfect opportunity to learn as much about the mouse-colored desert inhabitants as anyone, and he puts that knowledge to good use each year when he hunts them.

HUNTER BIO | EDDIE CLAYPOOL

EDDIE CLAYPOOL

AGE/HOMETOWN: 54/Chouteau, Okla.

YEARS HUNTING: 41 years

FAVORITE HUNT LOCATION: Arizona

DEER HARVESTED:
Probably over 100, with 38 that exceed the Pope and Young minimum – all 100 percent do-it-yourself.

LARGEST BUCK: 189 inches, 267 pounds.

FAVORITE METHOD:
Treestands and calling.

CONTACT INFO:
www.eddieclaypool.com

WHITETAIL SLAM: No

"How I hunt these deer depends entirely on the time of year. If I'm out in the early season when the bucks are still velvet-antlered and often in bachelor groups, I'm going to focus on water holes. Since I hunt public land, there is a lot of competition for the premier water holes, so I create my own. It's a ton of work, but I'll backpack in a 25-gallon tank and then replenish it with seven gallons of water about once per week. Once I establish the water tank I hang a camera on it and check it during the replenishing sessions. I've also had good luck with mineral licks and attractants in the early season but also keep an eye toward the natural food sources."

All of this sweat equity would lead you to believe that Stallone is a sit-and-wait style hunter, but that's far from the case. Instead, he's a hunter who will do whatever it takes to be successful throughout the entire season, although his go-to method for taking

HUNTING TIP

If you plan a do-it-yourself Coues deer hunting trip, you will want to take the pre-hunt planning seriously. The Desert whitetail can often be found at elevations from 5,000 to 9,000 feet, and they demand the ability to hike and climb just like a mule deer or elk hunt in many places. If you can't get to them, you can't kill them. Know beforehand the variance of terrain and what you're likely to encounter and then get in hunting shape for it. You'll be better off for the effort.

As you can imagine, 20-yard shots on Coues deer are not common for bowhunters. Instead, shot distances of 40 to 60 yards are much more likely, which necessitates a serious practice regimen and a total reliance on a laser rangefinder. For rifle hunters, a high level of accuracy is a must as well. Coues deer are small, cagey, and represent a challenge for even the most seasoned marksmen. If you set out in search of a Coues without first developing extreme confidence with your weapon of choice, you are probably setting up nicely for failure.

Do-it-yourself Desert whitetail hunter and Oklahoma resident Eddie Claypool killed this 104-inch deer in Arizona.

EDDIE CLAYPOOL

a Coues deer involves getting after them during the rut.

"I'm not the most patient person in the world and would much rather spot-and-stalk all day long. It's more proactive and although you can draw them in with rattling and some other eastern whitetail tactics, I just love the challenge of finding them with a spotting scope and then moving in on them. This is a tactic that is best suited for a two-man team so that one guy can sit on the scope and keep tabs on the buck and the nontarget does and direct the stalker."

Borrowed straight from the mule deer hunting handbook, Stallone's Coues deer style depends on several things. The first is that you and your hunting partner must clearly understand the hand signals and how to use them so that there is no question about what information is being portrayed from spotter to stalker. The second is that you must hunt with someone who understands the terrain you're in and how to read it. Many, many two-man stalks have ended up busted simply because the distance between hunter and deer was misjudged by the spotter. What looks like 200 yards from across the valley could be 100 yards in reality, and that information is key to the success of a stalk.

TOM MIRANDA

This six-point Coues buck just slipped under the fence. This buck won't make the Pope and Young record book.

HUNTER BIO | JOHN P. STALLONE

JOHN STALLONE

AGE/HOMETOWN: 37/Scottsdale, Ariz.

YEARS HUNTING: 32 years

FAVORITE HUNT LOCATION:
The Black Hills, South Dakota.

DEER HARVESTED:
46 in 15 different states.

LARGEST BUCK: 168 inches, 246 pounds

FAVORITE METHOD: Archery

CONTACT INFO:
Marketing Director and host of *Days in The Wild* for The Hunting Channel online:www.thehuntingchannelonline.com

www.facebook.com/john.stallone.52?ref=tn_tnmn

www.thewhitetailblueprint.com
secretsofhuntingwesterngame.com
mathewsinc.com/prostaffer/john-stallone

WHITETAIL SLAM: Yes

Beautiful Coues buck in Sonora's cattle country.

Before ever finding the chance to employ this method, you need to find deer. That's where Stallone's intimate knowledge of the area comes into play. "You need to look for certain features of the landscape that are likely to hold deer, and you also need to be able to recognize certain food sources while peering through your binoculars. That time of year barrel cactus, teddy bear cholla and prickly pear will either contain flowers deer like or fruit they are going to key on. Sometimes while you're glassing you'll notice a group of these plants that is bearing bright yellow or orange fruit, and you'll know the deer are probably going to feed there."

When hunting prey species like deer, learning as much about the plant life in the areas you plan to hunt is a good idea. Deer in all of the regions have a very diverse appetite, but will almost always key in on certain foods during specific times of the season. When you consider a desert environment, this becomes even more prevalent than a deciduous forest or a lush southeastern creek bottom.

All of the information he can glean on current deer habits is put to good use each day Stallone and his hunting partner set out to spot-and-stalk, however merely finding a tempting buck isn't good enough. "Stalk planning is extremely important. I'm meticulous about my scent, which is difficult in the desert because you're always sweating. I carry very minimal gear to reduce my burden and always plan my stalks around berms, ridges or other terrain features that will mask my approach. Also, if you're going to hunt the rut plan for the fact that the buck you're stalking is likely to be on the move. This is a time when you need to have absolute faith in your spotter and trust his judgment for guiding you into the exact spot the buck is going to pass through."

Even though Stallone is a resident of Coues deer territory, a lot of visiting hunters could learn from his tactics. Traveling with a trusted hunting partner is a great idea for anyone, especially when the foreign terrain can be dangerous. Secondly, working together with a like-minded hunter will certainly make things easier in the initial stages of the hunt when a divide-and-conquer method of scouting can be employed.

They are arguably the hardest of the Whitetail SLAM to tag out on, but that is part of the allure. Deer hunters are nothing if they are not at least a little competitive, and few feathers in your hat will garner as much respect as notching a Desert Coues on your quest to a SLAM. Naturally, if the DIY route isn't your thing, there are plenty of outfitters who specialize in Coues deer hunting. This can be a great option for hunters that want to glean first-hand knowledge of the land and the deer without sacrificing all of their vacation days.

CHAPTER 12

CHASING THE RUT: HUNT PLANNING

It's easy to talk a big game about traveling to such-and-such a place and hunting for whitetails, but the implementation of a road hunt requires attention to details lost on a close-to-home foray. To put it into perspective, think about the amount of gear a single whitetail sit usually requires.

First off, most of us hunt from a treestand. Depending on style, you're looking at a hang-on with steps or ladder sections, or potentially a climbing stand. Many of us opt for an all-out ladder stand in plenty of scenarios, although most models aren't conducive to traveling hunts. Beyond stands, there are calls of all sorts to consider. Rangefinders, binoculars, weapon and ammunition. Clothing and scent control products. Scents, decoys, knives, etc... The list could go on and on, and while each of us has our own system for gear organization, a long-distance hunt requires attention to detail so that you don't hike deep into a river bottom only to realize that your bow release is back at camp.

Long before ever putting a mile on your hunting truck, make a comprehensive list of the must-haves for a hunting trip. These are the things you carry on every hunt, no matter what. Then consider weather, time of year, rut stage and where you'll be staying. All of these factors will weigh on one end or the other of the scale, and all will determine what you should bring along.

TONY J PETERSON

If you travel in search of a SLAM buck during the rut, consider all-day sits. They aren't for everyone, but if you can tough it out you just might earn a shot at a midday cruiser.

A lip-curling buck is the quintessential rutting buck image.

ISTOCK

Knight & Hale's Pack Rack is an easy way to take rattling to the woods during the rut.

CHAD LENZ

Chad "The Savage" Lenz poses with a great Alberta buck. Careful planning can result in the whitetail trip of a lifetime that ends with a buck of this caliber.

Once you've got your gear readied, you'll need a method of transport. The best bet for the must-haves is to stow them in a daypack so that you know exactly where they are at all times. To better prepare yourself for a road hunt, use the same pack when you're hunting close to home so you familiarize yourself with it.

As far as clothing, plan for weather that might not be in the forecast. Many hunters have been burned by a quicker-than-predicted cold front, or warm front, or rainstorm, or "insert weather pattern here." Because of this it's necessary to be prepared – but not go overboard – so you can cover the what-ifs of a hunt.

Television host Melissa Bachman takes her what-ifs very seriously when it comes to out-of-state gear, specifically clothing. "For me it's all about comfort on the hunt. I need to be warm and comfortable because on just about any whitetail hunt my plan is to sit from dark to dark. This is nearly impossible if you're not prepared. I like to have a neck gaiter to keep the wind off

TONY J PETERSON

During the rut a buck can cruise by at any time of the day. If you can stomach an all-day sit – you just might be rewarded with a buck passing through when other hunters are having lunch.

KNIGHT & HALE GAME CALLS

Traveling to hunt whitetails involves an assessment of hunting goals and realistic expectations. We often focus solely on mature bucks, but shooting what makes you truly happy is never a bad idea, even if that means a deer like this small swamp-dwelling Wisconsin buck.

TONY J PETERSON

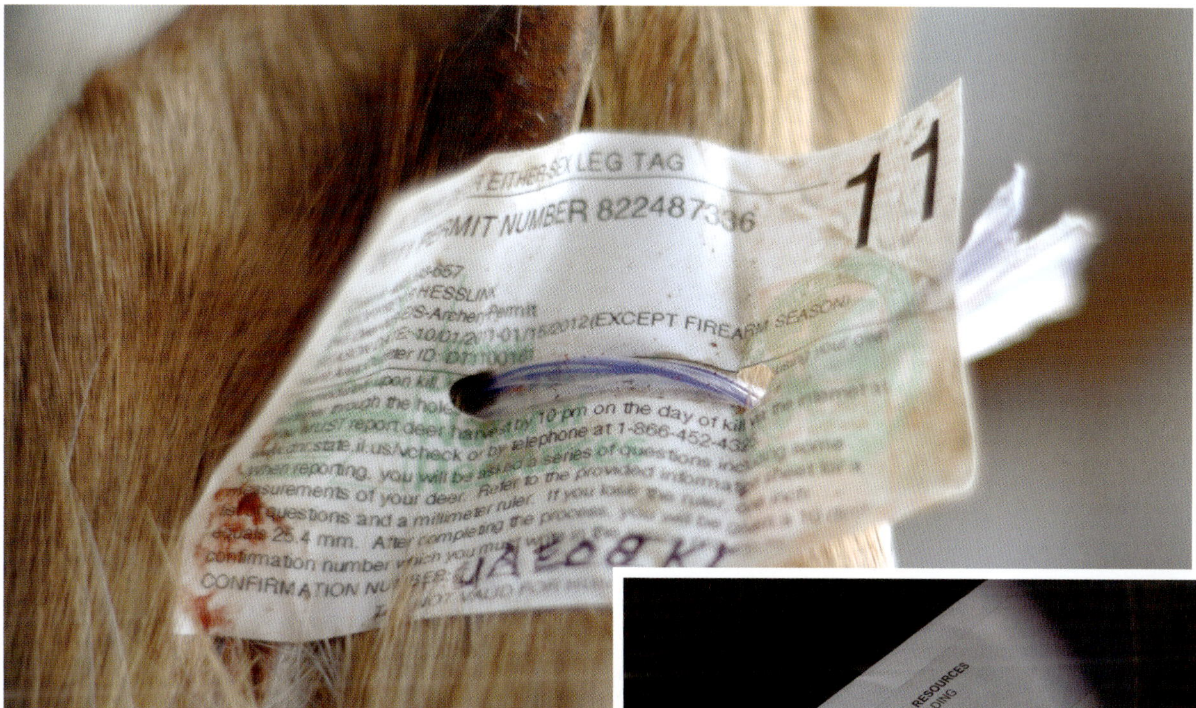

TONY J PETERSON

When you start planning your fall whitetail hunts, spend plenty of time researching the availability of licenses in your chosen areas.

TONY J PETERSON

SLAM hunters looking to visit the whitetail mecca that is Iowa should expect to wait two to three years to draw a tag.

of my neck and I use sticky heating pads on my kidneys in cold weather. I also rely heavily on a good cushion to sit on. If I'm not comfortable, I'm moving and that's bad. On top of that, when discomfort creeps in then it's much harder to enjoy the hunt, which takes away from the whole experience."

In the realm of traveling with weaponry, consider a backup if possible. Whether you're a bowhunter, muzzleloader hunter or rifle hunter, something can go wrong with your weapon. If that happens at home, it's an inconvenience. If it happens on the road, it can be a hunt killer. If you can't bring along an extra weapon at least bring some tools to work on your rig and arm yourself with the knowledge to make minor fixes. Bowhunters who have had a string loop or sight pin break on the first day of a hunt know this all too well.

Naturally, there is a lot to consider when it comes to hunting gear for any trip, but before you ever start packing it's necessary to figure out just where and how you can get a license.

A GAME OF TAGS

One of the most beautiful things about whitetail hunting is that, generally speaking, tags are readily available. There are exceptions to the rule, like the state of Iowa, that features certain zones that require two or three years of preference points before a nonresident can draw a tag.

Other big-buck states require a draw as well, but many are nearly guaranteed. Still others offer over-the-counter tags that can be purchased on site. With any potential hunt, it's absolutely necessary to research hunting licenses, which is something that is very common amongst western hunters. Colorado's Jace Bauserman knows all about this process and employs it to his

MARK WIMPY

HUNTING TIP: FULL BELLIES = HAPPY HUNTERS

Eating on the road can boil down to fast food and unhealthy options. If your destination hunt involves camping or staying in a hotel, consider cooking for yourself. A camp stove or a grill can be your best friend. Before the hunt, thaw venison strips or steaks and mix them in a bag with cut vegetables like peppers and onions. Add some butter or olive oil and seasoning. Make enough for all in your party and create a meal for each evening of the hunt. Once you return to camp or the hotel, simply dump the bag into a frying pan on your camp stove or the grill and cook it up. When it's nearly finished, add a bag of cooked rice. You'll feel better eating at least one quality meal each day.

advantage in the whitetail world.

"When I'm researching a whitetail hunt, I always check on availability of tags first. If I can buy an over-the-counter tag, then I know I can show up and get one. This means that I can watch the weather for the ideal time to travel, or can cater a hunt to that state around my busy schedule. Researching license availability also gives me the chance to plan out a more effective hunting schedule throughout the fall. If I know I'm going to get a tag in a state that might hunt better during the early-season, and one that should be dynamite during the rut, I can lock those in well ahead of time and start researching hunting locations."

Looking into potential whitetail states and identifying those that will ensure a tag also gives you a much needed backup should you come up short in a draw state. Hitting the road in search of whitetail hunting is something that gets into the blood and it's very hard to ignore the allure once you've done it. If you rely only on key big-buck states with tags that are difficult to obtain, you may miss out on hunting backup states that offer easy tags and incredible hunting as well.

Whenever possible, buy your tags before hitting the road. Just about every state allows you to purchase a license online, with some requiring nothing more than a credit card and a printer and you'll be set. Others will mail you a physical tag, which may take a week or more. Even if you're confident you can show up at a local Wal-Mart at midnight and buy your license, it's better to set out with the tag in your pocket whenever possible just in case. Otherwise, you could get there and

Mark Wimpy, of Illinois, has his Whitetail SLAM and is a "DIY" buck hunter.

PLAN FOR SUCCESS

Elk hunters seem to get it, but sometimes whitetail hunters don't. Planning for success is extremely important because once you get a deer on the ground; it's your legal and ethical obligation to ensure that none of the meat is wasted. Minnesota's Tony Peterson is almost religious in his obsession with caring for game while on the road, and he has a list of things he won't leave home without.

"I butcher all of my own game when I'm traveling to hunt so I always pack a gambrel to hang a deer up, several knives including a skinning knife, a knife sharpener, a bone saw, and box of Ziploc bags. I might not be able to fully break an animal down into freezer ready packages, but I can get a deer awfully close in a couple of hours. And more importantly, I get the deer cut up to the point where I can layer the meat in a cooler with ice and if I'm hunting in a camp, I can even start cooking the venison immediately. That's one of the reasons I love to cut up deer when I'm traveling."

Peterson's advice on prepping for a butcher session should serve anyone looking to piece out a big buck, but he also packs on other piece of gear. "About five years ago I started packing along a full-body bag that is designed to wick away heat. It's just like the bags that elk hunters use to carry quarters out, but large enough to fit over an entire deer and works perfectly for keeping flies, dust and debris off of the deer while it's hanging. This isn't as much of an issue in colder weather, but becomes a big deal on some of the early-season hunts where it's hot, buggy and dusty. I cover up the skinned carcass and only move it down to cut off another chunk of meat to work on. As soon as I've done that, I put the game bag on the carcass. This is a great way to keep meat clean and ensure that you don't have to rush the butchering process.

If going full-on butcher isn't your thing, make sure to locate a meat locker that will take care of your deer. Some hunters opt to donate their meat, which is a good choice as well but again requires a little planning. Depending on the state, some meat lockers charge even for donated meat; know ahead of time what will be expected of you.

As with any traveling hunt, consult the regulations before starting the butchering process or taking your kill to a locker. Laws vary greatly from state to state, and some allow for quartering or butchering without registration, while others require an on-site registration before anything can be removed from the carcass beyond field dressing.

TONY J PETERSON

Plan for success on your hunting trips. A full-body game bag is a great piece of gear to have, especially if you plan to butcher your harvest in camp.

find out something is wrong with the license printer, or that a certain store location doesn't handle license sales.

PLANNING TO BE PASSIVE (OR NOT)

During the planning phase, which coincides nicely with plenty of daydreaming about rut-crazed bucks cruising with their noses to the ground emitting guttural grunts with every footfall, the reality of how you are going to hunt should set in. Some hunters possess a great deal of patience, and should plan to sit all day – especially when the rut is cranking and it's possible to have an encounter during any part of the day. It's often touted, but not as often practiced, but all-day sits are the rule for rut hunting. Don't be lulled into a sit from dawn till 11 a.m., then lunch at camp, possibly followed by a nap, and then a 3 p.m. till dark sit from either the same or a different stand. Big bucks will move at midday and you can't shoot one in camp. Plus, although it can be oddly taxing to hunt whitetails day in and day out, the saving grace of a rut hunt is that the days are growing shorter. Your total commitment to sitting all of daylight will be a lot, but it's also a good time to go to bed early so you can stay fresh on stand all day long.

If you can't handle all-day sits very easily, consider moving from one stand to another with only a very short break in between. Transitioning between stands will break up the monotony and offer a fresh perspective on the day. Other hunters opt to read books or play games on their phones. This is a point of contention amongst hunters because some feel that it detracts from the hunt and is unnecessary. Whether that matters is up to subjective opinion, but if digging into a novel or playing Yahtzee on your phone will keep you out there all day, it's worth it.

If you still feel 11 or 12 hours in a stand will drive you batty, there is the possibility to go from passive to aggressive. Still-hunting through an area with the wind in your favor is a great way to pass the time. Although the method almost has a negative connotation now due to the fact that it's an easy way to spook deer, the reality is that it's a lot of fun and any buck taken this way is a true trophy.

Along the lines of being either passive or aggressive, if you witness good activity near your stand but realize you're not in the sweet spot, don't be afraid to move. Whitetail expert Stan Potts is one hunter who is not

HUNTER BIO | TIMOTHY KENT

TIMOTHY KENT

AGE/HOMETOWN: 35/Pittsford, N.Y.

YEARS HUNTING: 25

FAVORITE HUNT LOCATION: My home farms in western New York and south-central Ohio.

DEER HARVESTED: Over 50

LARGEST BUCK: 135 inches, 186 pounds.

FAVORITE METHOD: Bedding areas from a treestand.

CONTACT INFO: www.theory13creative.com

WHITETAIL SLAM: Not yet, but working on it.

HUNTING TIP: SLITHERY SURPRISES & OTHER DANGERS

By far the most dangerous aspect of deer hunting is climbing into and out of treestands. This should be a non-issue with today's offerings of harnesses and lifelines, but is still a major concern. Beyond the issue of gravity always winning, other dangers might await you on a traveling hunt. Catch a plane to South Texas and it's likely you'll have checked luggage containing snake boots. But what if you're going to western North Dakota? They've got plenty of rattlers, and if you don't do some pre-hunt research you just might meet one while unprepared, which is bad news. Safety on any hunt is a must, but when you're 1,200 miles from home with spotty cell phone reception – a slight misstep involving safety can turn into a major incident.

afraid to move if the best deer activity is occurring just out of his reach. "If I have a treestand hung anywhere that I feel is off of the mark, I'll get down and move. It doesn't do any good to sit there and second-guess your decision, especially if you're seeing deer doing something other than what you expected. Nine times out of 10, if you're moving you're killing because you have to be in the right spot. You have to be adaptable and willing to change."

This may seem like something that you can't plan for, but you can. If you go into a rut hunt envisioning a few key stands that will guarantee you a shot throughout the duration of your hunt, you might force something that is not working. Making something happen is not something every hunter is willing to do simply because it boils down to risk and reward, but the reward for being aggressive can be worth it.

This goes for the situations where you witness a buck either actually bedding down, or corralling a doe into a small patch of cover. There are times in every bowhunter's career when you see a mature buck locked down with a doe out of range. If the cover and wind accommodate, consider getting down and trying a stalk. Odds increase if it's windy, but often the doe will be intimidated by the buck, and if she hears or sees you she may not run. Better yet is the fact that the buck will be in breeding mode and at the dumbest point of his

It pays to research some of the dangers in the areas you plan to travel to. Shown here is a rattlesnake from western North Dakota.

TONY J PETERSON

Being realistic about potential success is essential on a traveling hunt. To up your odds, consider hunting with an outfitter, just make sure to call references and do your due diligence on any operation you're interested in.

TONY J PETERSON

The use of a four-point, rear-tether safety harness is a must for treestand hunting. This "Seat-O-The-Pants" model by Summit Treestands is tough to beat. Notice the heavy-duty locking carabiner.

life. Many huge bucks have been killed by aggressive hunters who climb down and stalk. Still many, many more have walked away never to be seen again by hunters who sat and hoped that the doe might walk in their direction.

This is a tricky situation, but if you're on a limited-time hunt and witness this situation, it's best to be honest with yourself. If you're not likely to see that buck again and the conditions are conducive to a stalk, go for it. Whitetails are highly stalkable; they just don't put themselves in a position to be spotted first very often. This means that most hunters only encounter this scenario a few times in their hunting careers and most don't possess the confidence to go after the buck.

PLAN FOR FAILURE

If you take a long look at the success rates for whitetail hunters, they will vary quite a bit depending on state and weapon. One thing you're not likely to see is 100 percent success, just as you're not likely to see zero percent success. Falling in the middle of that is the reality that for most hunts, you might have a 20 to 50 percent chance of killing. Those are just general though, and there are situations where the odds increase considerably if you're traveling to a tightly controlled property.

Reality, though, calls for a healthy dose of honesty and understanding that just because you have planned out everything perfectly, that doesn't mean you'll find yourself at the end of a short blood trail celebrating with your hunting buddies. Deer are better at surviving

Before you ever hit the road, consider that you might have to re-think your plan once you start hunting. Too many hunters play it safe and hunt passively, but if the deer are not moving near your stands it's best to move to where the action is hot.

TONY J PETERSON

than we are at killing them and that means most of the time they win. Throw in weather, moon phase, hunting pressure, predator prevalence and a plethora of other out-of-your-hands factors and it becomes a bit easier to understand why many states feature 30 to 40 percent success rates on all deer, not just mature bucks.

In fact, if more states published honest numbers on the amount of mature bucks killed per hunter, it would probably be disheartening. That however, is one of the greatest things about hunters as a whole – we are very optimistic. Even though a traveling hunt is a long-odds proposition, it's not impossible to step onto new ground and leave dragging a dead buck. It's very possible.

It gets easier with successive trips. If you're planning a hunt to a new area, realize that you might not be successful. You will learn plenty about the area though, and if you don't punch your tag this year, your odds will increase next year should you choose to return. This goes for any hunter who starts traveling in search of deer in new places, even if you never return to the same spots. Simply nailing down your travel lifestyle and equipment organization over a few trips will make you a better hunter. Plus, after a few trips to far-off places in search of a SLAM buck or two, you'll start to get into the groove and understand what it takes to win on the road. When you do get that first kill, it will further solidify what you've worked so hard to make happen.

New York resident Tim Kent has plenty of experience traveling in search of whitetails and has learned to keep an even-keel when it comes to success. "Sometimes you win, sometimes you don't. It really boils down to doing the best research and pre-hunt planning you can, and then hunting as hard as possible. If you do everything in your power to give yourself a chance and keep a good attitude along the way, the bucks will come and if they don't, that's okay. At least you will have known you tried to make it happen and it's only a matter of another trip, or another day and you'll get it done."

When done correctly, the planning phase of any hunt can be a lot of fun. It's not as enjoyable as the actual hunting, but the peace of mind that comes from knowing you've chosen the right state, secured a license, and picked the best dates for potential success, cannot be overstated. Top that off by mentally preparing yourself to hunt as hard as you'll need to, and that will make your whitetail trip all the better. Good luck!

HUNTER BIO JACE BAUSERMAN

JASE BAUSERMAN

AGE/HOMETOWN: 33/La Junta, Colo.

YEARS HUNTING: 11

FAVORITE HUNT LOCATION: South Dakota

DEER HARVESTED: 13

LARGEST BUCK:
136 inches, 200 pounds.

FAVORITE METHOD:
Spot-and-stalking and ground blinds on public land.

CONTACT INFO:
www.facebook.com/jmboutdoors

WHITETAIL SLAM: No

CHAPTER 13

HUNT SWAPS: THIS LAND IS YOUR LAND

America the Beautiful! The home of the brave, where spacious skies and amber waves of grain captivate our imagination as a nation, and are images that reflect the fact that we are the fortunate ones to be born on the most fertile and diverse natural paradise on the planet. This goes for all of our citizens, but is especially poignant for those of us who hunt.

Every corner of North America is blessed with the splendor of land, animals and a melting pot of cultures, which together have spawned a multibillion dollar travel and tourism industry. Land is perhaps the keystone of the American dream, and as we travel from the Atlantic to Pacific coast, or from northern Canada to the Mexican Sonora, it is in the changing landscapes that we see the reflections of our past, our dreams and our passions for the future.

As hunters, we are moved by the beauty of the North American landscape, yet we are more blessed than most in that we are entirely connected to the land. We manage it, improve it, and in truth need it as the core fiber that balances out modern life's often unhealthy diet of pastimes. We are the ones who keep the traditions of our heritage as stewards of the land. We are the ones who understand the relationships among wildlife, water, wheat and woodland, and the ones who both dream and live the reality of managing our land to the best of its potential.

The white-tailed deer is an American icon. It is a symbol of strength, endurance, survival and adaptation that is synonymous in many ways with our own struggles as we settled the land in the days of old, and now pursue life in a modern time when freedom and life are challenged in every way. These animals have adapted so diversely that they have inhabited nearly every acre of our continent. In the process, whitetails have captivated us so completely, that deer hunting has become an entire multibillion-dollar industry – all by itself.

When Woody Guthrie wrote the classic American song "This Land Is Your Land" back in the 1940s, in critical response to his feelings that Irving Berlin's "God Bless America" was superficial with respect to a nation in struggle, he was really on to something. That is, we can all clearly see that we are blessed with America's abundantly beautiful and fertile land, but that the real connection is in the way we use it, share it, steward it and enjoy it. In recent decades, land and more specifically access to the land, has become an increasingly hot topic among hunters. As more and more hunters began to recognize the intrinsic value in managing their own properties for older-age bucks, balanced sex ratios and an enhanced hunting experience, land and access have become scarcer and more expensive. The result is that hunters, whether in their home state or wanting to travel to experience hunting whitetails in far off places, now pay top dollar to have access to prime managed

TONY J PETERSON

If you're open to traveling during different times of the season, or hunting outside of the rut, you might run into a better opportunity to swap a hunt with someone in a different region.

TONY J PETERSON

ground through purchase, lease or outfitters.

Certainly times have changed, especially for those of us who can remember gaining easy access to hunting ground by simply knocking on a door and sealing the deal with a firm handshake. Nowadays, landowners spend so much time, energy and money managing the land for whitetails, that a knock on the door and request to hunt will likely be met with a resounding "No." There's a trust factor involved in not knowing whether a stranger will be a good steward, and also a fear factor that mistakes will be made in harvesting deer that don't meet the management plan of the landowner. The modern hunter is becoming more of a land and wildlife manager, and is keenly aware of the effects of pressure on the bucks they have been working so hard to identify, protect and grow to a mature age.

Despite the competition for top hunting ground, there are ways to find excellent opportunities for all hunters. Hunting whitetails across North America in pursuit of the Whitetail SLAM is an exciting and challenging experience that opens our eyes to the differences in the deer, the people, the culture and the experience. The habitat, terrain and genetic adaptations of bucks in different lands create a whole new adventure – and a whole new specimen than we can't get in our back-fourty. For those who dream of experiencing the ultimate whitetail hunting across North America, and becoming one of the elite hunters to have outwitted many different subgroups of whitetails and earned a Whitetail SLAM, there are options available to gaining access to some of the very best land available throughout the range of the whitetail.

OPTION 1: PUBLIC LAND HUNTING

Nearly every state has an abundance of public land available to hunters, and if you are a "do it yourself" hunter who likes researching, planning and executing hunts, this method can pay off big time both in cost and experience.

By far the most time consuming, but also the most cost effective, public land hunting is a great alternative to paying for outfitters or access. Modern technology, Google Earth, online topographic and property maps have made doing research on public hunting spots much easier than even 10 years ago. By adding a little common sense to technology, you can make that research pay off by putting yourself in the very best

HUNTER BIO | MIKE STROFF

MIKE STROFF

AGE/HOMETOWN: 32/Jacksonville, N.C., Uvalde, Texas

YEARS HUNTING: 25 Years

FAVORITE HUNT LOCATION: Illinois

DEER HARVESTED: Over 125

LARGEST BUCK: 186 inches, 350 pounds.

FAVORITE METHOD: Spot and stalk.

CONTACT INFO:
www.soehunts.com
www.savageoutdoors.tv

WHITETAIL SLAM: No

Bowhunter
MAGAZINE
SCENT BLOCKER

TONY J PETERSON

portion of those public lands. You'll increase your odds even more by leveraging the deer management practices of adjacent private lands.

Starting with the state you'd like to hunt, you can pull statewide public land maps. Narrowing the target area down to a quadrant of the state that is better habitat, or the type of hunting experience you desire is a crucial part of the first steps of planning. For instance, if you were looking into New York, the Adirondack Park has millions of acres available, big-bodied deer, and areas that likely never see a hunter all season – but it also has very low deer numbers. If you'd prefer to see two dozen deer a day, rather than one or two or none, you'd do much better to hunt the Catskill Mountain land where deer densities are higher than anywhere else in the state. Call the state department of natural resources office, or search online for past harvest reports by county, and you'll easily discover where opportunities are greatest.

Once you've narrowed your search down the common sense aspects come into play and it's time to begin looking at neighboring properties. Finding large tracts of private lands that are likely managed with food plots, cover, for older-aged bucks, and a higher density of both bucks and does is the goal. Using online aerial and topographic maps, you can then study the terrain to find likely funnels, ridges or bottoms where you're most apt to witness buck movement. Setting up closer to these properties gives you a greater opportunity to harvest deer, versus being in the middle of a public area where food, cover and overall hunting pressure reduces opportunity. Lastly, research the rut timing in that area to figure out exactly what week to plan your hunt, and ensure you are in the woods at the key time of season when the deer are moving most.

Also, you should leave two days prior to the start of serious hunting to get into the area, gauge pressure, look for stand sites, and do general scouting and preparation. Regardless of where, how or when you go hunt public land it will always be the lowest cost alternative, and can be truly cheap if you plan it correctly. Bowhunting writer Tony Peterson hunts several whitetail states every year and usually plans to camp for this very reason.

"I've stayed in motels and hotels on traveling hunts, but prefer to camp. It's cheaper and much easier because I can usually camp exactly where I want to hunt, which is important. I like being able to wake up and go without having to drive anywhere. I also like being able

A lot of hunters might pass on traveling to hunt public land because of the perception that they won't kill a mature buck. Shown here is bowhunting writer Tony Peterson with a mature Minnesota whitetail taken on public ground close to the Twin Cities.

Traveling hunts often necessitate lax scent-control standards, but toting along an in-the-field ozone generator can help greatly.

TONY J. PETERSON

Adam Hays with his 200-inch moose buck taken in central Ohio.

to grill in the evenings and even butcher deer in camp, which is not an option when you're headquartered in a motel.

"The downside of camping is that scent control becomes nearly impossible. This forces me to religiously play the wind, but in recent years I've been able to cheat some since I started using in-the-field ozone generators. They aren't magic, but they do buy you a much larger margin for error. I carry enough charged batteries to cover me during at least one evening or morning sit per day I plan to hunt. Sometimes the wind cooperates and it's not an issue, but other times I need to force it and the ozone generator helps considerably in those situations."

The logistics of pulling off a public land hunt can be mind-boggling, but if you break it down into bite-sized pieces you'll realize that it's quite manageable. Again, nothing comes easy on public land but that's okay. Just as some hunters prefer a recurve bow over a modern compound, or a flintlock muzzleloader over an inline model, the challenge of public land hunting has an appeal that cannot be denied.

OPTION 2: OUTFITTERS

The term "outfitter" is broadly used to encompass pay-to-play hunting, including self-guided hunts on land that owners charge a fee and allow DIY hunts. In its purest form, an "outfitter" is understood to provide full service lodging, meals, guides, land management, hunt planning and most importantly the expectation for an increased chance to harvest a buck. Top-flight outfitters unquestionably provide all of the above, BUT, the difficulty is that as in any business, all outfitters claim to be all-stars, and it's up to you (the buyer beware) to discover which one is best.

Horror stories abound at every deer camp about hunts gone wrong; thousands of dollars paid based on promises of bucks galore, 100 percent shot opportunities, excellent cooking and world class accommodations, all that turn afoul under the stark truth of reality as it triumphs over false promises. The fact is that many outfitters over-hunt their land, over-pressure their deer and over-harvest bucks. There is nothing worse than paying dearly for the unpleasant right to hunt in stands that are littered by last week's boot tracks and the odd cigarette butt. As we sit in these rancid thrones, the imagination can drift easily into wondering whether the hunters who left those tracks also spit chaw, drained bladders and left other scents of their presence behind.

This points to a two-way street between outfitter and client. Although there are certainly unscrupulous outfitters, there are also plenty of clients that make the entire process more difficult. It's important to remember that you're paying for the privilege to hunt certain ground with the expectation that the outfitter is going to try his hardest to get you a chance at a deer. Working with them and listening intently to your guide's suggestions is always well advised.

Savage Outdoors television host Mike Stroff knows all about the outfitter/client relationship. Stroff also owns and operates Southern Outdoor Experience (SOE) in Texas, and he sees his share of clients come through each year. "We try really hard to manage hunting pressure on our ranches, and do our best to ensure that each client is looking at fresh ground. I can also tell the hunters who take things seriously and aren't moving around or making noise because they will have action all day long. Others, who don't pay as close of attention can put down a stand site in a single sit. It's a tight-rope

TONY J PETERSON

Many Whitetail SLAM enthusiasts opt for outfitted hunts. While outfitters may promise the world, it's necessary to do your research before ever spending a dime to ensure you get the experience that you're paying for.

HUNTER BIO — CY WEICHERT, AKA "THE GRUNTMAN"

AGE/HOMETOWN: 47/Skaneateles, N.Y.

YEARS HUNTING: 34

FAVORITE HUNT LOCATION: Anywhere that has been well managed for wildlife in North America.

DEER HARVESTED: 34 bucks and well over 100 does.

LARGEST BUCK: 155 inches, 234 pounds.

FAVORITE METHOD: Mouth-calling

CONTACT INFO: www.ScoutLookWeather.com cy@scoutlookweather.com

WHITETAIL SLAM: No, but this year I head to Texas and Mississippi, and hope to attain it by the end of the 2013 season!

CY WEICHERT

Good outfitters rest their spots and rotate through a limited number of hunters to ensure the best hunt for everyone. Be sure to ask plenty of questions before booking a hunt.

walk because we can only do so much, it's still up to the client to stay still and make the shot when the moment comes."

There are thousands of outfitters to choose from, and from referrals, interviews, online research and talking to references the process to finally satisfy our doubts and finally booking a hunt is an exhausting one. In fact, finding those outfitters that are suitable brides for our own styles and expectations of hunting can be as difficult, or more difficult in some cases, than selecting the right public land to hunt. The key factor is that if you pick the wrong public land to hunt, and are let down by the results, you haven't also flushed several thousand dollars down the drain. Choosing one bad outfitter and having the hunt go bust leads quickly to a loss in money and valuable hunting time. This disappointment can taint a hunter away from outfitters forever.

To avoid such mishaps, many hunters have come to rely on booking services like Cabela's Outdoor Adventures, that offer top-notch outfitted hunts with no increase in cost over the outfitter's normal fees. The beauty of services like this is that their team of hunt consultants spends 100 percent of its time qualifying and vetting outfitters for their program. Cabela's is one of the oldest, most trusted names in the outdoor business and their service is rigorous in its selection process. All of the references are prechecked and the land has been hunted by their prostaff to ensure it will meet expectations. Accommodations, management style, land, guides, lodging and all other aspects of quality are set at the highest standards, and take over 90 percent of the research out of the process for you and nearly 100 percent of the risk, all at no additional cost. When you arrive at these outfits you can be sure that all is in place and on target with how it was sold to you. All you need to do is show up, enjoy your hunt and make the shot!

TOM MIRANDA

A NEW SOLUTION: WHITETAIL SLAM'S HUNTSWAP PROGRAM

There exists a third method of finding excellent hunting land, called HuntSwap, that is a solution to the pitfalls of both public land hunting and hunting with outfitters. HuntSwap is a free service of Whitetail SLAM, and is one of the great benefits of registering your buck(s) on whitetailslam.com. It allows like-minded folks the ability to hunt well-managed, private land in distant places by connecting and trading with other Slammers.

HuntSwap allows you to hunt on private land that is managed to standards and hunting practices that meet your expectations. Once you register your first buck on WhitetailSLAM.com, you can post your land for a

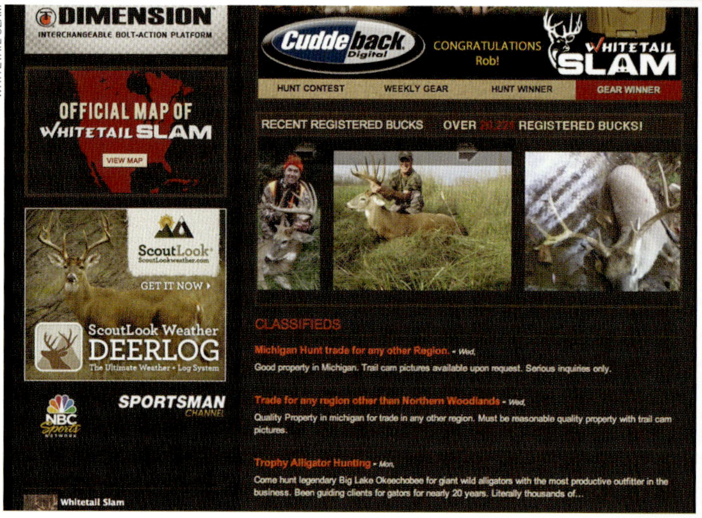

WHITETAIL SLAM

Hunters interested in visiting a new region with weapon-in-hand should look no further than the classified advertisements at www.whitetailslam.com. Here like-minded individuals offer up trading hunts between different regions.

Digital trail cameras like this Cuddeback have revolutionized big-game scouting, and allow hunters to share buck photos that include dated and time-stamped images.

TRAVELING HUNTERS SHARE A COMMON BOND

New York resident and deer hunting fanatic Cy Weichert has always marveled at the relationship that hunters share. He recalls experiences from his youth, "As a boy, my father took us hunting every weekend in the Adirondack Mountains of New York with an old Iroquois Indian man named Moses, who had traveled extensively when he was younger in his work as a railroad man. He often spoke of hunting in the southern mountains of Virginia and out in the Texas brush country, and one of his favorite things to say was 'I never met a whitetail I didn't love.' He spoke of getting out of work, strolling up to a homestead, rapping on the door to meet the landowner and asking permission to hunt. His stories were more about the great Americans he would meet, and the ones who had become lifelong friends who always welcomed him back to their lands and dinner tables in future years."

Although society has certainly changed since the days when Moses set out by rail and ended up hunting areas throughout the country, it's still very possible to find new places to hunt simply by being friendly and appreciative. Hunters share a common bond, and whitetail hunters especially relate to one another in a way that is rarely found in the world today.

swap with Slammers from another area, or post an ad looking to hunt somewhere new and wait for a reply. You can include a detailed description of your land, list all of the SLAM buck areas you want to trade for, specified states of choice and all other preferences, then connect privately with other Slammers to work out dates and details of your own swaps.

HuntSwap is unique by comparison to both public land hunts and outfitted hunts. Private land hunting is in many cases even better than hunting with outfitters, because pressure is oftentimes lower, and many landowners manage very well for quality herds. Verifying with the owner that he manages and hunts it the way you want is all part of the fun and the adventure. You begin building relationships that are mutually beneficial, as opposed to being "sold" by outfitters or being left "on your own" with selecting public lands to hunt.

Trading a hunt entails a level of trust. Both parties have the expectation that lands will be scouted properly and set up for the highest odds of success.

TONY J PETERSON

If you plan to trade a hunt with someone or simply travel to a new area, it might be necessary to hunt out of a camp.

Knowing you are going to hunt land that is managed and hunted in a way that meets your goals is a major plus. If you are like many modern landowners who try to protect all young bucks, then finding another Slammer who protects younger bucks means you'll be hunting an area that has more older bucks on the land. Knowing that you are going to hunt a place that is similar to your own property can bring a tremendous peace of mind as you embark for your trip. Like-minded people engaged in likewise land stewardship practices ensure that HuntSwap is one of the only ways you can be assured that the place you are hunting meets your expectations.

Harvest opportunity on private land is usually greater than public land due to less hunting pressure, but the real benefit is that you'll be certain that whenever you are set up in your stand there won't be another hunter on the upwind side of you, killing your chances to see any deer. This alone is enough fear for most hunters to never do a public land hunt.

Similarly, pressure on private land is usually far lower than outfitted land, purely due to the economics of it.

MOULTRIE FEEDERS

Where legal, supplemental feeding stations can help grow bigger bucks, bigger racks and supply hunters with venison for the table.

Outfitters need to put as many hunters on the land as they can to make their living. Private landowners make their living elsewhere, use their land as their own sanctuary for recreation, and typically won't over pressure the deer.

Hunting is one of mankind's most valuable methods of building camaraderie and friendships that endure over lifetimes and generations, but often our hunting buddies live in the same state as we do. A HuntSwap with another landowner from a far away state can provide the foundation for building new relationships with people from all over North America.

HuntSwap takes less time to select than private land hunts, costs less than outfitted hunts, and in reality will give you the highest possible chance for success. Also, the fact that you are going to hunt on land with the owner means there's no need for scouting and setting stands. Your HuntSwap host already knows the ropes, has stands set, knows where, how and when the deer move, and how the weather, wind and other factors affect the deer's habits in that area.

Ultimately, HuntSwap can offer all the benefits of an outfitter's knowledge of the land, but with less pressure and lower cash burn if your expectations are not met. The purest beauty of it all, though, is that HuntSwap builds a vested interest in your host to make your hunt as successful as it can be, so that when he comes to hunt on your land he knows he'll be getting the royal treatment in return. Log on to www.whitetailslam.com today and make HuntSwap one of the options for finding your next great place to hunt!

Whitetails change with the land and whether we lease it, own it, book on it with outfitters, hunt public parcels or swap it in pursuit of a Whitetail Slam. Somehow we are all carried off by it to the same exciting and peaceful place; the thrill of being up close to North America's wariest game, the satisfaction in accomplishing goals as a woodsman and hunter, and the experience of freedom that this great continent has to offer. We hunt them in the Northern Woodlands, the palmettos of Florida, in the shadows of Montana cottonwoods, on the windswept Dakota plains, on vast mesquite-brushed Texas landscape, and everywhere in between. No matter where it is, we always feel at home. This land, after all, is our land.

CHAPTER 14

HUNTING LEGACY

TONY J PETERSON

Few American hunters understand the level at which we each are blessed through our opportunities and heritage. Our continent was first explored by Spanish, French and British adventurers and the land was carved into New France, New Spain and New England. Those men, the forefathers to our way of life, thought nothing of exploiting the vast wildlife resources they found simply because the abundance was such that no right mind could envision using up what seemed to have no beginning and no end.

Expanses of forestland were leveled until what was once towering deciduous trees became cropland. Animals were slaughtered through subsistence and market hunting, which gained acceleration due to the establishment of railroads and their ability to ferry meat to rapidly growing cities. By the mid-1800s the industrial revolution was churning through previously rural ways of life to forever alter the even dissemination of humans and further congregate them into cities. As calendar pages turned, the endless reality of abundance became something altogether different and while it shrunk from a once indomitable entity, a few influential men began to read the writing on the wall. They too, had the sense to save it.

Men like Theodore Roosevelt, Aldo Leopold, George Shiras and William Healy Dall set their sights upon a similar course – to preserve what was once so taken for granted. Those men, along with other like-minded individuals brought hunting and conservation together in a marriage yet to be divorced. For the first time in our history, lands and wildlife would be managed for the wisest use, not the most immediate return.

TOM MIRANDA

Tom Miranda in early Realtree camo displaying one of his first whitetails shot on video. Circa 1992

The reason there are so many whitetails available today is because hunters are the orginal conservationists. Despite what the anti-hunting crowd claims, no group spends more time and money preserving deer than hunters.

TONY J PETERSON

North American hunters are envied by hunters from all over the world. No other place offers such easy access to lands and animals.

WISE USE

We all know of the prairies littered with countless bison skeletons, but to many of us that situation is abstract. That's because we've worked hard to rebuild those decimated herds and reverse the countdown to zero. The bison are an extreme example simply because of their once sheer numbers and the rapidity in which they were reduced to memory, but they aren't the only example of our shortsightedness with game. Elk, bear, deer and sheep have seen their way to the brink only to backpedal from near extinction to populations varied, but all successful.

Today's wildlife management extends into the 50 states, Canada, Mexico and all of Central America. It has expanded around the world because the stewards of wildlife understand that each animal has an intrinsic value. Not just a value as in or of itself, but as a value in the economy of the land for which it lives. Few things have greater value than what man desires, and game animals across so much of the earth have finally achieved a status of management meant to guarantee their survival.

Modern hunters, trappers and fisherman not only support wildlife management through wise use, but these individuals also give wildlife an economic value. For example, the huntable population of white-tailed deer in North America is valued at over one billion dollars in income annually. This money comes from hunters who purchase licenses and gear, as well as wildlife agencies that study the deer, and land managers who proliferate them. This value is why we have more deer now than when the pilgrims landed at Plymouth, and why we will continue to have deer, bears, elk and sheep.

That is also why it's so ironic that today's hunters are called murderers and zealots by animal protection groups. Even though hunters have been given credit for much of history's animal population demise, the fact is that hunters are the conservationists who also rebuilt them. In the days of early conservation, men like Theodore Roosevelt, Saxton Pope, Frederick Courtney Selous, Jack O'Connor and other hunting icons and conservation heroes were mocked and degraded by

The chance to hunt whitetails is a gift, make sure your legacy consists of an appreciation of the sport and every attempt possible to be ethical while passing on the tradition to anyone who is interested.

TONY J PETERSON

Registering your buck harvest with organizations like Whitetail SLAM is a great way to preserve your hunting legacy.

ERIC RAIN

groups of activists. Roosevelt hunted Africa to provide the Smithsonian with specimens; Selous shot over 500 specimens for the Natural History Museum in London. In those days darting and radio collaring wasn't possible and animals were harvested in the name of science. Some were mounted for display in museums.

Those men, like so many of today's hunters, represent what the anti-hunting crowd despises. We are a living representation of what nature does because we opt to do just what nature intended, but somehow are supposed to be better than what we are. The anti-hunters look to us as the dregs of society because we enjoy our pursuit of the white-tailed deer and other game animals, but would never acknowledge that we love to be outdoors for the sake of it. Certainly, we enjoy a short blood trail and the silent thanks given to a freshly taken animal, but that is one piece in a much larger mosaic.

We don't kill solely for fun, nor do we take an animal's life because of something dark hiding inside of us. We do it because of what we are, and we want to work hard for that privilege and do not take it lightly. As history has proven, we will just as soon lay down our weapons to allow a game species to rebound, as we will grumble over a lost opportunity. No one in society

Here Tom Miranda poses in his "good luck" New Jersey Devils jersey with his desert sheep and archery Grand Slam award plaque.

spends as much as us on animals, and no one cares as much. No birdwatcher, no anti-hunter, no one.

We are the ones that ensure game animals exist year in, year out.

GET INVOLVED

Today, we are fortunate to have organizations of hunters that help to keep a perspective on hunting and join together outdoorsmen of like mind, ambition and cause. Where some look at trophy hunting only in the negative connotation, our perspective is different and rightfully so. To look into the membership roles of organizations like the Safari Club International, Grand Slam Club or Pope and Young Club is to look into the vault of hunters who are willing to stand up for the needs of wildlife conservation. They are ever willing to put their hard-earned dollars into the support of wildlife management and the heritage of hunting.

Hunter conventions generate money for wildlife. Where else can you attend an auction and watch hunters bid into the tens and even hundreds of thousands of dollars for a specific license or tag to hunt an animal? Special tags offer bidding hunters a chance to hunt inside protected park boundaries or refuges and the opportunity to take a magnificent trophy. Hunters who pay big dollars in these auctions do so because they have a passion for hunting and a means to financially give back to the sport they know and love. These dollars give wildlife real value and are earmarked to wildlife management, research and habitat.

Hunting organizations conduct raffles, form committees and conduct fundraisers all in the name of conservation. These same groups work to protect hunting privileges as well as work with state game departments on hunting seasons and fair regulations. Avid hunters contribute valuable data to help biologists study wild animal populations, diseases and dynamics.

The hunting we all love has never been free. From the times when all of us were young and hunting pheasants with our fathers, the roosters that flushed from those lands were owned and managed by farmers who had money and time invested to have wild birds on their property. Those landowners left crops for feed and nesting cover. They managed their land for the balance of nature and wildlife at their own expense and let us hunt their land.

Times have changed, yet some things stay the same. Hunters still love the land and the wild creatures they pursue. Hunters still cherish their heritage and look upon hunting with a respect to wildlife. When once there was a time when land was valued only upon its ability to grow crops or trees, now it is also looked at as habitat and its ability to carry wild animals. These added values come as a result of hunting and conservation efforts.

TOM MIRANDA

Group photo from the 2011 archery Super Slam awards presentation in Las Vegas, Nev. These are some of the best bowhunters on the planet.

TOM MIRANDA

A 1994 image of ESPN TV personality Tom Miranda posing with a great Northern Woodlands buck.

Consider how you can carry on the hunting heritage. As a member of these valued organizations, you are a part of an elite fraternity of hunters. There are many ways to give back to your hunting heritage – like attending a school classroom and doing a talk on hunting and wildlife conservation. Endowments such as a will, trust or life insurance policy with a hunting organization as a benefactor can be additional ways to fund organization efforts when your hunting days are over.

HONOR YOUR LEGACY

Registering your big-game animals into the record books and for the Slam awards is an important step to-

Hunting is often a solitary sport but doesn't always have to be. If you choose to get involved in organizations like Pope and Young and SCI you can meet other like-minded individuals.

TONY J PETERSON

Passing down the hunting tradition is an important part of anyone's hunting legacy. Here, bowhunting writer Tony Peterson poses with his father Jared. Tony arrowed this nontypical in Minnesota in 2006.

ward preserving your hunting heritage. The documentation of these animals and the adventures in which you pursued them is also instrumental in building your personal hunting legacy. Registering your accomplishments archives them and validates you as an ethical and responsible hunter. Belonging to hunting and conservation organizations provides opportunities to donate time and funds to support projects that promote youth hunting, wildlife habitat and conservation initiatives.

Consider writing articles about your hunting adventures and take sharp, clean photos of your animals, and keep these documents stashed away. In time they will become the personal memoirs of your hunting career – something that you likely have no time to do if you think of it like that! Yet, your family will appreciate the effort and enjoy reading your stories and adventures in later years.

Think about attending hunter conventions and getting more deeply involved in the organizations. Buying hunts and raffle tickets at hunter conventions not only helps the organization, but also the outfitters, wildlife and the future of hunting.

The opportunity to obtain licenses and hunt throughout the vast range of whitetails in North America is a privilege hunters should work hard to maintain.

TONY J PETERSON

This photo shows Tom Miranda's Super Slam award certificate and the 54 separate hunting licenses he purchased to take the 29 North American big-game animals with a bow. These bowhunts are documented on video and can be seen on his *Adventure Bowhunter* DVD available at tommiranda.com.

DOCUMENTING IS EASY

Keeping your old, expired hunting licenses is another step toward archiving your hunting legacy. Those licenses prove that you hunted the animal with a legal license, and in many cases they provide dates of harvest, state and county of take – and more. I keep my licenses in zip lock bags and archive them by species and date.

Field photos are also important, so try to get a nice, clean photo of you and your trophy before field dressing. Noting pertinent facts like shot distance, tracking distance and a few additional high points of the hunt is also valuable information.

I urge every hunter to take a class and become a SCI, P&Y or B&C measurer.

Not only can you measure your own animals for gross score, but also learning to measure will make you a better judge of trophy quality in the field.

Registering the animals requires an official score and then a signed affidavit and a fee. The process can be tedious, yet the steps ensure accurate record books and help to deter dishonest entries. Most organizations require the signing of a "Fair Chase" statement, which means that the animal was taken by the individual using methods and ethics that are honored by the club. The goal of these record books is to honor the magnificent animals and the hunters who took them.

Slam entries need not be scored trophies, but Slams require field photos as well as a harvest affidavit. Slams are often categorized by the weapon used like archery, muzzleloader, pistol or crossbow. Four bucks constitute a Whitetail SLAM, but four bucks all taken with a bow is an archery Whitetail SLAM. The bow hunts make an archery SLAM a much more difficult feat and worthy of special recognition.

Often hunters make excuses why they don't register their animals or belong to organizations. Arguments are that hunters hunt for themselves, for meat on the table, and not to hang horns on the wall or tout their hunting achievements in public. These ideals are the demise of hunting. Think of it as the old trapper who

CONTACT INFORMATION

Name

Address

City

State/Province Zip/Postal Code Country

E-mail

Phone

SUPERTEN™
OF NORTH AMERICAN BIG GAME

To qualify for the **SuperTen of North American Big Game**, you must have at least one from each of the ten categories listed below. To apply, provide the information below, along with a hunting photo of each species, to Grand Slam Club/Ovis. GSCO dues are $60 annually. It is not necessary to have taken any trophy animal to be a member of GSCO.

BEARS	❑ BLACK BEAR ❑ GRIZZLY BEAR	❑ ALASKA BROWN BEAR ❑ POLAR BEAR *Choose one.*	Date Taken / Location (Please be specific) Outfitter / Booking Agent Contact Information
CATS	❑ COUGAR	❑ JAGUAR (pre-1972) *Choose one.*	Date Taken / Location (Please be specific) Outfitter / Booking Agent Contact Information
DEER	❑ WHITETAIL DEER ❑ COUES WHITETAIL DEER ❑ COLUMBIA BLACKTAIL DEER	❑ MULE DEER ❑ SITKA BLACKTAIL DEER *Choose one.*	Date Taken / Location (Please be specific) Outfitter / Booking Agent Contact Information
ELK	❑ ROCKY MOUNTAIN ELK ❑ ROOSEVELT ELK	❑ TULE ELK *Choose one.*	Date Taken / Location (Please be specific) Outfitter / Booking Agent Contact Information
CARIBOU	❑ MOUNTAIN CARIBOU ❑ WOODLAND CARIBOU ❑ CENTRAL CANADIAN BARREN GROUND CARIBOU	❑ QUEBEC LABRADOR CARIBOU ❑ BARREN GROUND CARIBOU *Choose one.*	Date Taken / Location (Please be specific) Outfitter / Booking Agent Contact Information
MOOSE	❑ CANADA MOOSE ❑ ALASKA YUKON MOOSE	❑ SHIRAS MOOSE *Choose one.*	Date Taken / Location (Please be specific) Outfitter / Booking Agent Contact Information
BISON / MUSKOX	❑ BISON	❑ MUSKOX *Choose one.*	Date Taken / Location (Please be specific) Outfitter / Booking Agent Contact Information
GOAT	❑ AMERICAN MOUNTAIN GOAT	*(required)*	Date Taken / Location (Please be specific) Outfitter / Booking Agent Contact Information
ANTELOPE	❑ PRONGHORN ANTELOPE	*(required)*	Date Taken / Location (Please be specific) Outfitter / Booking Agent Contact Information
SHEEP	❑ DALL SHEEP ❑ STONE / FANNIN SHEEP ❑ DESERT BIGHORN	❑ ROCKY MTN. BIGHORN ❑ CALIFORNIA BIGHORN *Choose one.*	Date Taken / Location (Please be specific) Outfitter / Booking Agent Contact Information

Submit this application along with a hunting photo of each species to: **Grand Slam Club/Ovis**, P.O. Box 310727, Birmingham, AL 35231

This form is used to document animal species for a hunter pursuing the Super Ten of North American Big Game.

One of the kindest things anyone can do is introduce a newcomer to deer hunting.

tells no one of his methods and then takes his secrets to the grave. Sure he may have been more successful than a trapper who shared his go-to tactics and intricacies of trap-set, but to whose benefit does that become over time? Like the burning libraries of ancient Rome, lost knowledge is perhaps one of the most shameful things we can be a part of.

Involvement in organizations by registering animals and species Slams is a way to give back, to be involved and proliferate our sport – not to hoard it for personal reasons. Reading about hunts and looking at trophies is how youngsters get interested, and sharing experience is how we all learn. We owe it to our forefathers and the wildlife to be involved. Besides, I'll bet each of us will continue to learn more about ourselves and the animals we love by being involved. It's the right thing to do.

FINAL THOUGHTS

This book is titled *The Rut Hunters*, yet it's really a tribute to all who pursue, protect and proliferate whitetails. North America's whitetails are truly amazing and they continue to expand their range. Whether a hunter pursues bucks only at home or sets a course to travel and pursue his or her own Whitetail SLAM, the opportunities to learn more about deer and the benefits of an outdoor lifestyle abound.

The hunters featured in this book are dedicated hunters who walk the walk with ethics and responsible hunting practices. Many of them have chosen careers in the outdoors; some promote hunting and wildlife management at the highest levels of learning. Others are just die-hard hunters who love the challenges that come with each new whitetail season.

TOM MIRANDA

Three lifelong buck hunters and best friends. L-R: Tom Miranda, Stan Potts and Joel Snow pose in an Ohio woodlot with Miranda's Union County buck.

It may be easy to write off those included in the pages of this book, but bear with me. Many, myself included, are lucky to experience hunting that is out of reach for some. I understand that, but make no apology for working my way through plenty of bleak years to end up where I'm at today. I'm dang proud of that, as many of the featured hunters in this book are, however I don't want to get too far way from my roots.

That is why I'm so passionate about this project, and the Whitetail SLAM in general. Deer are God's gift to all of us, a true living representation of the fortune each one of us experiences upon each waking day. What better thing is there than to know you can hunt each day of the season for such a creature? Or better yet, set a course with your hunting buddies for new adventure a few states away? In the grand scheme of things, very, very few people are as lucky as whitetail hunters. We have our passion and the means to engage in it. Not to mention we have the conviction to preserve our opportunities, and the heart to pass them on to those looking on with curious eyes and a willingness to match wits with a whitetail. Some days it seems too good to be true, but it's not. It's real and that is beautiful.

It is my hope that the contents of this book become a catalyst to your future hunting endeavors. That the tactics and strategies described herein bring you to deeper thought in your own hunting efforts and success finds it's way into your deer camp, and better yet, when success eludes you that you still find solace in the comfort of a treestand.

Understanding that each of us is a small but essential piece to the overall dynamics of today's hunting world makes each and everything we do an important part of its future. Don't take your hunting privileges for granted. Start now to document your hunting legacy and begin to do your part to ensure hunting continues for your children's children. In the grand scheme of life hunters are the stewards of the earth's wild creatures. What you do now, today and tomorrow will affect how hunting and wildlife survive into the next century. What a wonderful burden to shoulder...

Hunt hard, don't quit, and enjoy every second of it.

SPECIAL THANKS

Mitch Kezar/Windigo Images

MITCH KEZAR — *Photographer*

Twice nominated for the Pulitzer Prize in spot-news photography, photographer Mitch Kezar has shot in the frigid depths of Lake Superior for *National Geographic*, trailed presidential candidates across the country for *Time* and *Newsweek*, spent days in sub-zero temperatures shooting ads for snowmobiles, traveled with natives across Africa, and ridden trains across China with peasants and chickens, all in search of the perfect image.

Today his work is heavily outdoor-sports related. He is a regular contributor to *Outdoor Life, Field & Stream, American Hunter, Bowhunting World, Sporting Classics* and many other hunting and fishing industry publications. Mitch is the founder of Windigo Images, a Minnetonka, Minn.-based stock photo agency, which is the world's largest image library specializing in hunting, fishing and outdoor subjects.

www.kezarphoto.com

John Hafner

JOHN HAFNER — *Photographer*

John Hafner is a Montana-based photographer and writer. He works with many of the top manufacturers, magazines and retailers in the hunting industry, and travels the globe shooting ad campaigns and catalogs for his extensive client list. It's rare to find John anywhere but behind his camera, but when not shooting images or writing copy, he enjoys family time with his wife and two dogs, and trading his camera for a little time behind the gun in the whitetail and turkey woods.

www.johnhafnerphoto.com

DALLEN LAMBSON — *Artist*

Dallen Lambson was born March 4, 1977 to Hayden and Cheryl Lambson in Pocatello, Idaho. He was the third of eight children and has always felt blessed to grow up in a large family. "It was a nice arrangement," he said. "Everyone had someone to beat up on." Dallen has always considered his family and upbringing to be a significant influence for good in his life.

A husband and father, Dallen spends much of his time sharing an art studio with his father producing oil paintings that depict his passions – wildlife and the great outdoors. He creates his graphite pencil work at his home in Pocatello. When he's not painting or drawing, he enjoys time with his family, hunting, fishing and fulfilling church callings. Dallen's artwork can be found internationally at various retail stores including Cabela's, Bass Pro Shops, Gander Mountain, Sportsman's Warehouse and others.

www.lambsonart.com

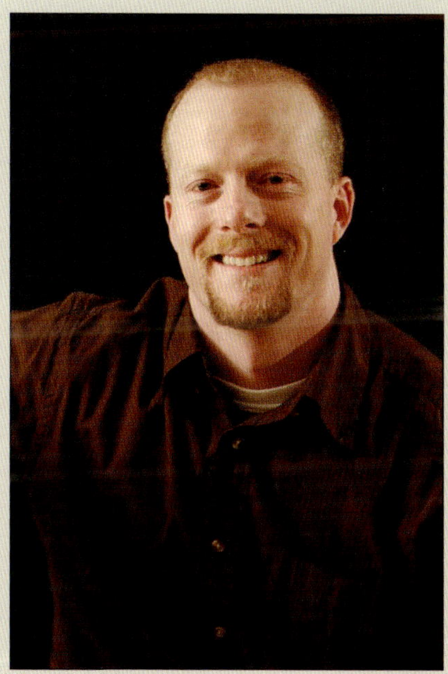

Dallen Lambson